Instructor's Guide

Ninth Edition

HARBRACE COLLEGE COLLEGE HANDBOOK

Instructor's Guide

Ninth Edition

HARBRACE COLLEGE HANDBOOK

Mary E. Whitten
North Texas State University

and

Eileen B. Evans
Western Michigan University

Harcourt Brace Jovanovich, Inc.

New York / San Diego / Chicago / San Francisco / Atlanta
London / Sydney / Toronto

ISBN: 0-15-531838-1

Preface

This Instructor's Guide, like the Handbook it accompanies, combines the virtues of a reference work with those of a textbook. As a reference for occasional consultation by instructors, the Guide includes:

—answers to all exercises in the Ninth Edition except those that call for original work

—supplemental class activities, arranged by Handbook section, intended to help stimulate student interest in various aspects of language use

—a select bibliography of current works of interest to teachers of composition

As a "textbook," the Instructor's Guide offers the following background material:

—brief, practical discussions of each of the thirty-four sections in the Handbook

—suggested criteria for the evaluation and grading of student themes

—annotated sample pages of Forms 9A and 9C of the *Harbrace College Workbook*

In addition to the Instructor's Guide, the *Harbrace College Handbook* is accompanied by a number of auxiliaries:

Correction Chart / An instructor's correction chart, which is an enlarged version of the front endpapers of the Handbook, is available free of charge to all adopters. Many instructors find the correction chart a convenient reference for marking papers; for that reason, it is frequently posted on a nearby bulletin board.

Harbrace College Workbooks / Users of the Handbook are encouraged to supplement it with one of the three forms of the *Harbrace*

form of the Workbook follows the organization and numbering system of the Handbook. And in each form, the examples and exercise material are thematically arranged (sports in Form 9A, animals in Form 9B, and the world of work in Form 9C) to provide continuity and stimulate interest in the material. Each Workbook comprises roughly two-thirds exercise material and one-third explanatory material; pages are perforated so that completed exercises can be easily removed and handed in to the instructor. A two-color Instructor's Edition of each Workbook is available to adopters of the respective Student Edition. (The Instructor's Edition is identical to the Student Edition, except that answers to all exercises are overprinted in red ink in the appropriate spaces.)

The *Harbrace College Workbook* can be used to supplement the exercises in the Handbook; it can also be used as a free-standing and completely self-sufficient text. Some instructors ask all students to purchase the Handbook, and only those students needing extra help to purchase the Workbook. It is important to note that Form 9A and Form 9B are virtually identical in explanatory matter, differing only in the theme of the exercises. In short, Form 9A (available now) and Form 9B (available in 1983) are interchangeable alternates.

Form 9C differs from Forms 9A and 9B not only in its special theme—the world of work—but also in its more extensive coverage of basic grammar. Approximately one-half the exercise material in Form 9C is devoted to basic grammar, the remainder to the other five parts of the Workbook. Another difference is that the explanations in Form 9C are written more simply than their equivalents in Forms 9A and 9B.

Test Package / Available on request to all adopters of either the *Harbrace College Handbook* or one of the three forms of the *Harbrace College Workbook* is a new, expanded Test Package, containing two test booklets, test answers, two template overlays, and a set of instructions. The tests are designed for efficient scoring and diagnosis, with each question relating to a particular section in the Handbook or Workbook; student weaknesses can therefore be analyzed and remedied with speed and accuracy.

The Test Package contains a total of 400 test items, with 200 designated as diagnostic (intended for use early in the term) and 200 as achievement (intended for use at the end of the course). Each set of 200 items is further subdivided into two tests of 100 items each, for classes where shorter tests are desirable. Each booklet contains two answer-sheet masters, with space for 100 responses each. The templates are intended to be placed directly over each student answer sheet. If the student has answered a test item correctly, the pencil mark will show through the hole of the die-cut template; otherwise, no mark will show, and the response can be counted as an error.

The Test Package is provided to instructors and departments free of charge, as a service to users of the *Harbrace College Handbook* or the *Harbrace College Workbook.* Accordingly, the Test Package contains a copyright notice allowing photocopying of test booklets and answer sheets without further permission from the publisher. All uses other than those intended are prohibited without written permission from the publisher.

Syllabi / The regional sales offices have been supplied with a variety of syllabi correlating the *Harbrace College Handbook* with several readers and literature anthologies published by Harcourt Brace Jovanovich. Instructors wishing to obtain copies of these syllabi or answers to any questions relating to the *Harbrace* package are invited to write to the nearest regional sales office (addresses are included on the back cover of this Guide) or to write or call their local HBJ College Department sales representative.

Contents

Sections 1–34: Discussions, Activities, and Answers to Exercises   1–127

Criteria for Evaluating and Grading Themes   128–30

Annotated Selective Bibliography   131–42

Annotated Sample Pages   143
Harbrace College Workbook, Form 9A   144–47
Harbrace College Workbook, Form 9C   148–49

Sections 1-34:
Discussions, Activities,
and Answers to Exercises

1 Sentence Sense

Grammar instruction shows students the patterns of English and provides part of the common vocabulary students and instructors use in discussing the strategies of effective sentences and paragraphs.

Defining both *grammar* and *usage* and distinguishing between them alerts students to the importance of both the system of and attitudes toward the English language. After quoting definitions of *grammar* from several abridged dictionaries ("the system of word structures and word arrangements of a given language at a given time"—WNWD), you might read the following definitions to the class:

> "The science of language is philology, or, in more recent jargon, *linguistics*. Grammar is a branch of that science, and can be defined as the branch that deals with a language's inflections (*accidence*), with its phonetic system (*phonology*), and the arrangement of words in sentences (*syntax*)."
>
> —H. W. Fowler, *Dictionary of Modern Usage,* 1965

> "A linguistic description of some language is called a grammar of that language. A grammar, then, is a set of statements saying how a language works. It includes, for example, a description of the principles for combining words to form grammatical sentences."
>
> —Ronald W. Langacker, *Language and Its Structure,* 1968

You could then read the definitions of *grammar* in W. Nelson Francis's "Revolution in Grammar" (*The Quarterly Journal of Speech,* October 1954, pages 299–312), in order to show the distinction made between grammar and usage.

ACTIVITIES

1. After explaining the concepts of sentence expansion, reduction, and combining (see Section 1, pages 3–4), provide a few short sentences for expansion and for combining. Then dictate one long sentence (or write it on the board) for students to reduce to basic parts.

2. A word's part of speech is determined by its use in the sentence. Have students write sentences to show:

> *down* as adverb, adjective, preposition, verb
> *well* as noun, verb, adverb, adjective, interjection
> *outside* as noun, adjective, adverb, preposition
> *near* as adverb, adjective, verb, preposition
> *like* as verb, noun, preposition, adjective, adverb
> *that* as adjective, pronoun (demonstrative and relative),
> adverb, conjunction

3. Ask students to form two sentences, using the words below. Use the results to discuss the importance of word order in English.

Sentence 1: camping, gear, handing, is, Kate, Marcia, the
Sentence 2: and, beside, forlorn, fountain, Jennifer, lost, sitting, studied, terrier, the, the

Possibilities for Sentence 1:

> Kate is handing Marcia the camping gear.
> Marcia is handing Kate the camping gear.
> Is Marcia handing Kate the camping gear?
> Is Kate handing Marcia the camping gear?

Possibilities for Sentence 2:

> Jennifer, lost and forlorn, studied the terrier sitting beside the
> fountain.
> Sitting beside the fountain, Jennifer, lost and forlorn, studied
> the terrier.
> Jennifer studied the lost and forlorn terrier sitting beside the
> fountain.
> Lost and forlorn, the terrier sitting beside the fountain studied
> Jennifer.

4. Have students eliminate prepositional phrases from the follow-ing sentences and then identify subjects and verbs. Deleting prep-

ositional phrases reduces the number of nouns and, thus, the number of possible choices for subject. For additional practice, have students use such sentences as 8 and 10 of Exercise 3 in Section 1.

a. Among my collection of houseplants over the past five years, strawberry begonias remain a favorite above all others.
b. According to horticulturists, the strawberry begonia is neither a strawberry nor a begonia in spite of its name.
c. In its natural habitat the plant produces runners which creep across the ground in search of a place to anchor miniature plants.
d. With the exception of overwatering and overfertilizing, an indoor gardener past the age of reason can make few mistakes in the tending of these plants with hairy, variegated leaves.
e. Once, however, I did uproot an entire plant during an attempt to remove a dead leaf near the edge of the pot; because of that unfortunate mistake I've been more cautious about grooming plants since then.

5. Some suffixes that signal nouns are *-ation, -hood, -acy, -ism, -ence, -ance, -ness, -ment, -ship, -ity, -age, -dom.* Some suffixes that signal verbs are *-ize, -ify.* After introducing some of these suffixes, ask students to supply suffixes for the following words and make any necessary changes in spelling:

foot (footage)	code (codify)
incline (inclination)	secrete (secretion)
liquid (liquidate, liquify)	rely (reliance)
bright (brightness, brighten)	public (publicize, publicity)
lunar (lunacy)	note (notation, notify)
lively (liveliness, livelihood)	kin (kinship)
opportune (opportunity, opportunism)	
plural (pluralism, plurality, pluralize)	

Note: *-er* to signal nouns (*teacher, driver, baker*) carries the meaning "one who"; *-er* to signal verbs (*glimmer, flutter*) carries the meaning "recurrent or frequent action."

Ask students to think of other suffixes that signal verbs and/or nouns, to invent nouns and verbs using these suffixes, and to provide definitions for these made-up words. For a useful treatment of suffixes, see Norman C. Stageberg's *An Introductory English Grammar* (3rd ed., Holt, 1977). Stageberg discusses source verbs with derived nouns, source nouns with derived verbs and adjectives, and source adjectives with derived verbs and nouns.

6. Have students identify each verb as *transitive active* (TA), *transitive passive* (TP), *intransitive linking* (IL), or *intransitive complete* (IC) and then identify any objects (DO, IO), or complements (SC, OC).

        TA   DO   OC

a. Ruth considers herself a scintillating conversationalist.

                     TA   DO

b. In fact, however, she monopolizes conversations at every opportunity.

                             TP

c. What unpleasant topics of conversation should be avoided during meals?

                                 TP

d. Gossip about friends and complaints about neighbors have been banned by Dale and Gwen.

                         IC

e. After seven years of marriage Gwen still frowns at Dale's comments about a neighbor's untrimmed lawn or cluttered sidewalk.

          IL   IL

f. He always seems contrite afterwards and becomes even more talkative in order to restore tranquility.

       TA   IO   DO   TA

g. Gwen beams him her approval, and the two of them resume

                    TP

eating while the day's news is reviewed on the evening news-

              IL

cast that has become an articulate dinner guest.

                   IC

h. Neither Gwen nor Dale can relax during dinner as long as the

           TP

nightly news is left on.

        IL

i. Still they are proud of their rules for pleasant mealtime conversation.

7. Have students use the present-participle form (the *-ing* form of verbs) as a verb in a verb phrase, as an adjectival (participle), and as a noun (gerund):

      He was *playing* the villain. [verb in verb phrase]

The man *playing* the villain is Joe. [participle in adjective phrase]

His role is *playing* the villain. [gerund in noun phrase]

Suggested verbs: *dive, press,* and *babbling*

8. Ask students to provide past participles (adjectives) describing their reactions when:

   a. a two-hundred-dollar tax refund arrives in the mail [*relieved sigh, elated squeal*]

   b. an instructor asks a question on material that the student has not read yet [*embarrassed mumble, fabricated excuse*]

   c. a personnel director calls to offer a job interview

   d. inclement weather forces the university to close for a week

   e. the last parking space in the lot is taken by someone on a moped

9. Ask students to compose a sentence with three infinitives that name activities or goals for the year after graduation, goals or activities within five years of graduation, and reasons the goals may not be achieved.

10. Have students identify each word according to function and/or part of speech:

    a. If Kris has been a Steelers' fan for years, why does she want to see the Eagles play?

    b. Selecting a most unusual name for her cat, Rachel called him Zeus, but when Zeus had kittens, Rachel chose another name—Zenobia.

    c. Really! That's a likely excuse coming from such conspicuous consumers.

    d. Planning a holiday party becomes more exhausting every year; but as soon as our guests leave, we will probably begin to plan another one.

    e. Heavens! If your cheese soufflé flops, we can always eat cauliflower or some extremely tasty muffins that were baked yesterday.

11. To review the various forms of sentences (simple, compound, complex, compound-complex) have students spend a class writing a paragraph on the board. The amount of board space will determine the number of paragraphs. Hand pieces of chalk to the first group of volunteers and ask each of them to create a simple sen-

tence. Make no comment. Ask the students as they finish to hand the chalk to their replacements, who are then asked to continue the paragraph (usually, but not always, narrative) with a compound sentence. Repeat the process until sentences of all types are written for each paragraph. Then read each paragraph aloud, asking students to check the sentence for correct form and to revise when necessary. This approach relieves the routine of exercises and promotes camaraderie, especially when done on Friday as a review of sentence types.

12. Ask students to identify any objects in these two sentences:

> Harold handed the huge ham to *Helen*.
> Harold handed *Helen* the huge ham.

Students who equate function and meaning may identify the italicized words as indirect objects. To clarify the difference here, you may want to point out the presence of *to* in the prepositional phrase and the position of *Helen* as indirect object. Omitting *to* from the first sentence would produce *Harold handed the huge ham Helen;* adding *to* to the second would create a prepositional phrase after the verb:

> Harold handed *to Helen* the huge ham.

13. Have students identify the verbal phrases and explain the function of each:

a. *Having spent most of March at professional meetings,* he welcomed a quiet weekend at home. [participial—modifies *he*]
b. At last I have typed a page without *making an error.* [gerund—object of preposition *without*]
c. It was impossible *to determine who was telling the truth.* [infinitive—subject of *was;* expletive *it*]
d. Brent, *dejected and frustrated,* spent the day by himself in the park. [participles—modify *Brent*]
e. *Aesthetically appealing* apartments *to be rented by undergraduates on a modest income* are a rare find. [participial and infinitive—modify *apartments*]

14. Have students pick out the infinitives and infinitive phrases (I, IP), participles and participial phrases (P, PP), and gerunds and gerund phrases (G, GP) in the following sentences:

                                       P   P

a. Who would guess that Winthrop with his *rumpled* suit, *tousled*

                   P

hair, and *unassuming* manner was a philanthropist who de-
                   GP

lighted in *befriending undergraduates at his alma mater?*
    PP   IP

b. *Ambling across campus,* he would stop *to chat with students
    as they relaxed between classes.*
                          IP

c. In an effort *to discover what students thought,* Winthrop
                            PP

    would listen carefully, *noting their informal evaluation of
    courses and instructors.*
      IP   IP   GP

d. *To assess these students' ability to solve problems by applying*
                                  IP

    what they learned in classes, Winthrop would lead them *to argue
    the merits of space colonization.*

e. The coherence and the logic of the defense were just as impor-
                            P

    tant as the solutions *being defended.*

f. When a student particularly impressed Winthrop, he offered
     IP   IP   GP

    *to help finance his or her college career by paying one semes-
    ter's tuition.*

            PP   IP

g. *Not wishing to have his identity revealed by his signature on a.*
                 IP   P

    check, he liked *to hand the amazed student cash at the end of
    the conversation.*
     IP

h. *To be truthful,* few students had probably realized the benefits
         GP

    of *communicating clearly.*

15. Have students compose sentences that contain the elements spec-
ified below:

a. adjective clause; noun clause
[*She knew that this woman who sat before her had tried many
criminal cases.*]

b. adverb clause modifying verb; noun clause as direct object

[*As Margaret listened to the witness, she realized that her client had not divulged all the facts.*]

c. adverb clause modifying adverb; adjective clause
   [*Margaret's calm reaction, which surprised me, was more restrained than even I had expected.*]

d. noun clause as indirect object; adverb clause modifying verb
   [*Send whoever is treasurer this bill from the caterer before we are charged a late fee.*]

e. noun clause as direct object; noun clause as appositive
   [*The fact that the landlord has doubled the rent means we must look for another apartment.*]

Because sample sentences for this exercise are time-consuming to write and to grade, they are better used as an in-class activity. Students may bring their completed sentences to class for discussion and evaluation.

ANSWERS TO EXERCISES

■ **Exercise 1** (p. 8)   **Underlining verbs and subjects**

	Subjects	*Verbs*
1.	friendships	develop
2.	Secrecy	was
3.	Rodgers	courts
4.	fire	gobbled up
5.	Answers	may be found
6.	vitamins	are
7.	television sets	are
8.	simplicity	gave
9.	Gnats, flies	invade, pollinate
10.	He	straightened, breathed, swung

■ **Exercise 2** (p. 13)   **Underlining objects**

1. —
2. problem [SC]
3. trouble
4. some
5. —
6. important [SC]
7. —

8. actions, force
9. sheath, blossoms
10. glasses, prayer, hoe

■ **Exercise 3** (p. 13)   **Labeling subjects and complements**

1. argument
2. Inventions; hallmark [SC]
3. people
4. Homer
5. people; useless [OC]
6. intelligence, integrity
7. America; kind [SC]
8. multitude; ignorant [OC]
9. enemy
10. idiot

For Class Discussion: Sentence patterns and verb classification

1. argument bruises myths
   SUBJECT + VERB (trans. act.) + DIRECT OBJECT

2. Inventions are hallmark
   SUBJECT + VERB (intrans. linking) + SUBJECT COMPLEMENT

3. people fled
   SUBJECT + VERB (intrans. complete)

4. Homer gives us information
   SUBJECT + VERB (trans. act.) + INDIRECT OBJECT
      + DIRECT OBJECT

5. people find nothing useless
   SUBJECT + VERB (trans. act.) + DIRECT OBJECT
      + OBJECT COMPLEMENT

6. Intelligence, integrity can be imposed
   SUBJECT (compound) + VERB (trans. pass.)

7. America has been kind
   SUBJECT + VERB (intrans. linking) + SUBJECT COMPLEMENT

8. multitude is making us ignorant
   SUBJECT + VERB (trans. act.) + DIRECT OBJECT
      + OBJECT COMPLEMENT

9. enemy is
   SUBJECT + VERB (intrans. complete)

10. idiot would press button
SUBJECT + VERB (trans. act.) + DIRECT OBJECT

■ **Exercise 4** (p. 19)   **Classifying words according to part of speech**

   pron. *v.* *prep.* *adj.* *n.* *prep.* *adj.* *adj.*   *n.*
1. He struts with the gravity of   a frozen penguin.

   n. *v.* *adv.*   *v.*   *prep.* *n.* *prep.* *adj.* *n.* *conj.* *conj.*
2. Men are often taken, like rabbits, by the ears. And though

   adj. *n.*   *v.* *adj.*   *n.*   *pron.* *v.*   *adv.*   *v.*   *n.*
  the tongue has no bones, it   can sometimes break millions

  prep. *pron.*
   of   them.

    adj.   *v.* *adj.*   *n.*   *prep.* *adj.* *adj.*   *n.*
3. Awesome is the tyranny of the fixed idea.

  prep. *adj.*   *n.*   *n.*   *v.* *adj.* *adv.*   *adv.*   *adj.*
4. Of all persons, adolescents are the most intensely personal;

  pron./adj.   *n.*   *v.* *adv.*   *adj.*   *prep.* *n.*
   their   intensity is often uncomfortable to   adults.

(Note: *their* may be classified as a pronominal adjective.)

  pron. *v.* *adj.*   *n.*   *conj.* *adv.* *prep.* *adj.* *n.* *pron.* *v.*
5. They pick a President and then for four years they pick

  +*particle* *pron.*
    on   him.

(Note: *pick on* may be classified as a phrasal verb equivalent in meaning to *criticize*.)

■ **Exercise 5** (pp. 22–23)   **Underlining gerund and infinitive phrases**

1. Successfully merchandising a product
2. to know the point of it all
3. enforcing strict new anti-litter laws
4. Taking criticism from others
5. Merely to argue for the preservation of park land
6. to fight back
7. giving birth
8. to pipe the gas through a purifying plant and into a pipeline

9. even saving a stranger from drowning
   donating a million dollars to the poor
10. growing plants without soil
    to attract amateurs' attention

■ **Exercise 6** (p. 24)   **Underlining and classifying phrases**

1. <u>like that one</u>   adjective
2. <u>blinded by the sun</u>   adjective
   _____   adverb
3. <u>Crawling through the thicket</u>   adjective
   _____   adverb
   <u>of shells left on top of the truck</u>   adjective
   _____   adjective
   _____   adverb
   _____   adjective
4. <u>to watch closely</u>   adjective
   <u>ruling behind the political scenes</u>   adjective
   _____   adverb
5. <u>racing along the beach</u>   adjective
   _____   adverb
   <u>over our big sand castle</u>   adverb
6. <u>on that ticket</u>   adjective
   <u>in the balcony</u>   adjective
7. <u>to college</u>   adverb
   <u>to get a liberal education, to learn a trade</u>   adverb
8. <u>one man sawing logs</u>   adverb [absolute phrase]
   _____   adjective
   <u>the other loading the truck</u>   adverb [absolute phrase]
   _____   adjective
9. <u>Not wanting to appear in court</u>   adjective
10. <u>All told</u>   adverb   [absolute phrase]

■ **Exercise 7** (pp. 27–28)   **Finding and classifying subordinate clauses**

1. that modern processing often robs food of its natural color—*noun clause*
2. What my son wants to wear or be or try to be—*noun clause*
3. whose basic attitudes are drastically changed—*adjective clause*

4. As I talked to my neighbors—*adverb clause*
   that all of them did depend on a world that stretched far beyond
   their property lines—*noun clause containing adjective clause*
5. As it declines in value—*adverb clause*
6. If a pitcher who throws only a fastball and a curve ball is in a tight
   situation—*adverb clause containing an adjective clause*
7. as people often believe—*adverb clause*
   Because a trail so often hangs several inches or sometimes feet
   above the ground—*adverb clause*
   even if he wades through water—*adverb clause*
8. that involve processing words—*adjective clause*
9. which all but assumes the role of parent, or teacher, or lover—
   adjective clause
10. what it is, what you want it to be—*noun clauses*

■ **Exercise 8** (p. 30)   **Identifying main and subordinate clauses**

1. <u>Practice never really makes perfect</u>, and <u>a great deal of frustration
   invariably accompanies juggling</u>.
2. <u>Nature is his passion in life</u>, and <u>colleagues say</u> [he is a skilled
   naturalist and outdoorsman].
3. <u>The two clouds have a common envelope of atomic hydrogen gas</u>,
   [which ties them firmly together].
4. <u>Transportation comes to a halt</u> [as the steadily falling snow, accu-
   mulating faster [than snowplows can clear it away], is blown into
   deep drifts along the highways].
5. <u>Agriculture is the world's most basic industry</u>; <u>its success depends
   in large part on an adequate supply of water</u>.
6. [Probably because their whirling sails were new and strange to
   Cervantes], <u>windmills outraged the gallant Don Quixote</u>.
7. <u>There have been several attempts to explain this rhythm</u>, but
   [when each hypothesis was experimentally explored], <u>it had to be
   discarded</u>.
8. <u>Allegiance to a group may be confirmed or denied by the use or
   disuse of a particular handshake</u>, [as Carl's experience indicates].
9. <u>Some black stem rust of wheat has been controlled by elimination
   of barberry, a plant</u> [that harbored the rust].
10. <u>We know</u> [that innocent victims have been executed]; <u>fortunately,
   others condemned to death have been found innocent prior to
   execution</u>.

■ **Exercise 9** (p. 30)   **Classifying sentences**

1. compound
2. compound-complex
3. complex
4. complex
5. compound

6. complex
7. compound-complex
8. complex
9. complex
10. compound-complex

■ **Exercise 10** (pp. 30–31)   **Identifying clauses; classifying sentences**

1. *Main clause:* Jim angrily called himself a fool
   Subordinate clause: as he had been doing . . . swamp
   Complex
2. *Simple*
3. *Simple*
4. *Main clause:* He had enough mysteries . . . sort
   Subordinate clause: which involved . . . values
   Complex
5. *Main clause:* now he was chasing down ghosts
   Main clause: this chase . . . was absurd
   Compound
6. *Simple*
7. *Main clause:* The legends had horrified him as a child
   Subordinate clause: that surrounded the ghosts
   Main clause: they were a horror still
   Compound-complex
8. *Subordinate clause:* As he approached the dark trail
   Subordinate clause: that would lead him to . . . mansion
   Main clause: he felt almost sick
   Complex
9. *Simple*
10. *Main clause:* Only this grotesque night seemed . . . real
    Subordinate clause: whatever ghosts might be . . . shadows
    Complex

■ **Exercise 11** (p. 31)   **Converting sentences to different structures**

Answers will vary. The following are possibilities.

1. a. Having smuggled marijuana into Spain, the men were sentenced to six years in prison.
   b. The men smuggled marijuana into Spain; they were sentenced to six years in prison.

   c. Because the men had smuggled marijuana into Spain, they were sentenced to six years in prison.

2. a. First condemning the property, the council then ordered the owner's eviction.

   b. The council first condemned the property; then it ordered the owner's eviction.

   c. After the council had condemned the property, it ordered the owner's eviction.

3. a. Applying for a patent on his invention, Uncle Oliver learned of three hundred such devices already on the market.

   b. Uncle Oliver applied for a patent on his invention; he learned of three hundred such devices already on the market.

   c. When Uncle Oliver applied for a patent on his invention, he learned of three hundred such devices already on the market.

4. a. Carefully examining passports and luggage, the border guards delayed every tourist.

   b. The border guards delayed every tourist; they carefully examined passports and luggage.

   c. The border guards delayed every tourist as they carefully examined passports and luggage.

2   Sentence Fragments

The fragment, the comma splice, and the fused sentence are serious errors in formal writing because they violate the reader's expectation that the writer will use grammatically complete sentences, punctuated as such. In addition, fragments may hamper the reader's comprehension of ideas. The students who make these errors show that they are unable to control the structure of an idea. Further, since an inability to control structure reflects an inability to control ideas, the reader may question whether the writer can control the content. Finally, students who cannot recognize units of complete thought and write them as such will doubtless have trouble limiting a topic, defining an issue, and developing ideas.

ACTIVITIES

1. Have students distinguish fragments from sentences by using ads found in popular magazines, such as the following (from an issue

of *Ladies Home Journal*):

a. Set yourself free. With Stouffer's.
b. Save a Lettuce's Life. (General Electric)
c. Improving on the French. (Stouffer's)
d. California Avocados. Only 17 calories a slice.
e. And you thought Ethan Allen just made great furniture.
f. The Benson's 'new' Faribo wool blankets are still in use. One Great Depression, one World War and One Golden Anniversary later.
g. Less is More. (Ivory Liquid)
h. Why No-Wax Floors Need Help. (Brite)
i. The first dry dog food that's like a home-made meal. (Gravy Train)
j. Introducing Cutex Nailcare. Because great-looking nails don't just grow that way.
k. Wonderfully flavorful vegetable combinations, in a special light sauce that lets each unique taste come through. Delicious. (Green Giant)
l. The Fisher-Price Riding Toys. Because your kids have more energy than you know what to do with.

Discuss what reasons might justify the use of fragments in ads (discourse aim, limits of space, need to attract interest quickly, etc.) or how the use of fragments affects a reader. From the items above have students identify the grammatical structures used as fragments (if necessary, suggest the categories: prepositional phrase, verbal phrase, dependent clause, adjective, appositive, adverb). Finally, have students collect fragments from their favorite magazine ads and label the grammatical structures of those fragments.

2. Have students number from 1 to 20 on a piece of paper. Then dictate ten short sentences mixed with ten fragments. Students should write down each word group and write S or F after each.

3. Give each student a copy of the following collection of fragments. Caution students to read the entire passage before they begin to rewrite it. Doing so will help them to plan their strategy for including all of the ideas as smoothly as possible.

Celebrating birthdays as an occasion for a family get-together. A summer barbeque or a winter buffet at Aunt Leah's. The oldest child and only daughter in a family of eight. Because planning a meal for forty-seven relatives requires the cooperation of every family involved. Certain relatives bringing their traditional specialties. To be sure. Potato salad from Aunt Catherine and corn relish from Aunt Meg. With Uncle Frank's contribution being the favorite. Pecan pie for dessert. Although there is no birthday cake and no one ever sings "Happy Birthday." To celebrate birthdays just the same.

ANSWERS TO EXERCISES

■ **Exercise 1** (pp. 35–36)   **Eliminating sentence fragments**

1. novels, such as science fiction
2. home, earnestly seeking
3. sarcasm or to make
4. His beard was gone and his hair was cut.
5. old and to speak of
6. soon—maybe next month
7. effect, not only on
8. A few minutes later a news bulletin
9. His face was turning redder by the minute.
10. That is against the law of averages but possible.

■ **Exercise 2** (p. 37)   **Eliminating sentence fragments**

1. a try after I had grown tired
2. to college and that all tests
3. spring fever, which
4. blood and whenever
5. advertisements that use

■ **Exercise 3** (p. 38)   **Eliminating sentence fragments**

1. That closet is the worst disaster area on campus.
2. It is even worse than ignorance.
3. plans, and they decided
4. ground and lowers them
5. It was a feeling that I could not analyze.

■ **Exercise 4** (pp. 38–39)   **Finding and revising fragments**

2. information, not just
5. In all probability, it takes
7. This statement seems
8. to me, to say

10. whiskers and that
11. feet, if my math
12. Some other interesting facts are
14. Another birthday would not be
15. the year 2004 because

3 Comma Splice and Fused Sentence

Students who frequently write comma splices or fused sentences are so busy trying to get their ideas down while simultaneously modifying or clarifying them that they lose sight of the strategy for a particular sentence. Failure to remember the structure at the beginning of the sentence may result in a fused sentence; an afterthought may result in a comma splice.

Incomplete structures or tacked-on sentences are best treated by drawing examples from students' writing and explaining why the errors might have happened. Once students see how the process has gone awry and which of their composing habits they must watch in the future, it is time to offer ways to correct the sentences; for students who have some insight into the ways of writing are usually more attentive to suggestions about writing. Teaching punctuation alone does not correct the practice of writing a comma splice or fused sentence. Students need to understand that planning sentences, selecting ideas for emphasis, ordering ideas, and revising force them to pay attention to structural details; and that as attention to structure increases, the number of comma splices and fused sentences should decrease.

ACTIVITIES

1. Have students replace coordinating conjunctions between main clauses first with conjunctive adverbs and then with transitional phrases, making any necessary changes in punctuation. Encourage students to vary the placement of conjunctive adverbs and transitional phrases. Refer students to rule **23a** and to the list of conjunctive adverbs in Section **31**, pages 367–68.

   a. Molly enjoys giving presents to her friends and relatives, so she shops all year long for clever gifts.

b. Last month she surprised her five-year-old nephew with a roll of transparent tape, and she gave him a box of fluorescent chalk for his drawing projects.

c. Candles are one of her favorite inexpensive gift ideas, yet a single candle costs more than five dollars.

d. Molly solves that problem by pouring her own candles, and she has made seven vanilla-scented ones and three frosted ones recently.

e. To receive one of Molly's candles is to be delighted, for Molly is as patient in her candle-making as she is clever in her gift-giving.

2. Ask students to correct the faulty punctuation between main clauses in the following sentences:

a. In high school Laura decided that she would become a research physicist, in fact, she even knew what area of research—cyrogenics. [physicist. In fact, OR physicist; in fact,]

b. She excelled in her physics class; yet her trigonometry and algebra teachers kept telling her that her math skills would never be strong enough for her career. [class, yet]

c. She listened attentively to their warnings because she assumed that teachers were expert judges of a student's potential in all fields, the fact that she always had the highest grades in physics did not influence her as much as the opinions of two teachers. [fields; OR fields. The]

d. Laura abandoned her career in physics and chose another career equally demanding now she is excelling in her study of econometrics. [demanding. Now OR demanding;]

ANSWERS TO EXERCISES

■ **Exercise 1** (p. 43)   **Linking sentences**

Answers may vary in the choice of the coordinator.

1. a. hunting; he
   b. hunting, but he
2. a. game; she
   b. game, and she
3. a. him; she
   b. him, so she
4. a. screen; we
   b. screen, and we

■ **Exercise 2** (p. 44)   **Linking sentences**

Answers will vary in the choice of the subordinating conjunction and in the position of the subordinate clause.

1. When Dexter goes hunting, he carries
2. Because the stakes were high in the political game, she played
3. Since the belt was too small for him, she had to
4. At the drive-in, while they watched the musical comedy on one screen, we enjoyed

■ **Exercise 3** (p. 44)   **Proofreading**

A checkmark should follow sentences 1, 5, 7, 9, 10.
An *X* should follow sentences 2, 4.

■ **Exercise 4** (p. 44)   **Revising comma splices or fused sentences**

Since various methods of revision are called for, answers will differ. The following are samples.

1. hard. Everyone
2. microbes; those microbes
4. Because . . . failed, some
5. automobile, yet the war
7. night. By morning
9. mournfulness; it
10. labor. Some

■ **Exercise 5** (p. 47)   **Connecting sentences according to a pattern**

1. The art company . . . paintings; however, the work . . . omitted.
2. The loud arguments . . . convincing; therefore, the majority . . . motion.
3. I . . . money; after all, he . . . cousin.
4. India . . . poor; as a matter of fact, it . . . reserves.

■ **Exercise 6** (p. 47)   **Dividing quotations**

1. "I . . . again," wrote Kenneth Bernard. "In fact . . . again."
2. "I . . . prejudice," W. C. Fields once said. "I . . . equally."
3. "I am . . . sing," Artemus Ward commented. "So are . . . me."
4. "What . . . marsh?" Gene Marine asked ironically. "Who . . . swamp?"

5. "There is . . . art," Pablo Picasso states. "You must . . . something. Afterward . . . reality."
OR
"There is . . . art. You must . . . something," Pablo Picasso states. "Afterward . . . reality."

■ **Exercise 7** (p. 48)   **Revising comma splices and fused sentences**

Answers will vary. The following are samples.

1. says, "You're
3. Johnny. Besides
4. home. In Oklahoma
6. William, who
8. right, for that happy marriage
9. Illinois. There
10. attack; however, Nellie's arteries
11. sweetheart. Then
12. want it to. Age is

■ **Exercise 8** (pp. 48–49)   **Revising sentence fragments, comma splices, and fused sentences**

Revisions may vary. The following are samples.

1. only; then
2. people. A family . . . now, not to mention
3. relay; however
4. year. It
5. ✓
6. work. The reason is
7. ✓
8. botulism. This
9. It is an argument riddled with stupid assumptions.
10. I usually buy . . . paperbacks, although I never get . . . them.

4   Adjectives and Adverbs

Students who have mastered the identification of adjectives and adverbs in written sentences yet who sometimes use one for the other as they write may be relying on their spoken language for their word choices. As a result, words that are heard in conversation (whether or not they are correct) are assumed to be appropriate in written discourse as well, and the student produces ''a prejudice referee'' or ''ice melts slow,'' or sentences such as those in Exercise 2.

Students need to understand that in both writing and speaking there are levels of formality (see Martin Joos's *The Five Clocks*). What may be acceptable in casual, daily conversation among friends is not acceptable in a job interview; what is acceptable in a journal or diary is not acceptable in an essay examination. Once students identify the audience and the appropriate level of formality, they can more readily observe the conventions for that level, whether in speech or writing, and can better understand that the advice to ''write like you talk'' rarely applies to formal English.

ACTIVITIES

1. Have students consult their dictionaries for the comparative and superlative forms, if any, of:

Adjectives		
articulate	friendly	little
base	frizzy	morose
far	graceful	ready

Adverbs		
contritely	loudly	soon
early	often	very
likely	quite	well

   Ask students to write sentences for three of the adjectives in comparative form, and for three of the adverbs in comparative or superlative form.

2. Ask students to write sentences using each of the following: *graceful diving, diving gracefully, hurried eating, eating hurriedly, gleeful laughing, laughing gleefully.*

   Because the gerund has properties of both verb and noun, students may have some trouble deciding on correct modifiers. The following sentences can serve as illustrations:

   She is known for *her rapid answers*. [adjective + adjective + noun]

She is known for *her rapid answering.* [adjective + adjective + gerund]

She is known for *her answering rapidly.* [adjective + gerund + adverb]

She is known for *her answering questions rapidly.* [adjective + gerund + object + adverb]

Answering rapidly, she defended her vote. [participle + adverb]

Answering the questions rapidly, she defended her vote. [participle + object + adverb]

In the adjective + gerund construction, the adjective tells *what* or *which* about the gerund. In the gerund + adverb construction, the adverb answers *how* or *when* about the gerund.

3. Ask students to distinguish between subject and object complements in the following sentences:

   a. The traffic committee's recommendation to triple the fee for on-campus parking stickers proved unpopular.
   b. You can label his argument illogical only if you can identify the errors in his assumptions.
   c. The waves of laughter from the audience made the comedian happy.
   d. Jim and Mary always say that their toddler is hyperactive, but the pediatrician always pronounces him healthy and normal.
   e. As the warm front moved through the state, the evenings turned balmy.

4. As a class activity, have students identify the adjectives and adverbs in a paragraph from a recent theme. Then have students, working in groups of three or four, revise the paragraph by adding, deleting, or substituting adjectives or adverbs. Ask someone in each group to read the revised paragraph to the class.

ANSWERS TO EXERCISES

■ **Exercise 1** (p. 52)   **Converting adjectives to adverbs**

1. answered vaguely OR vaguely answered
2. traveled safely OR safely traveled
3. fought fiercely OR fiercely fought
4. refused quickly OR quickly refused

5. welcomed heartily OR heartily welcomed
6. conformed blindly OR blindly conformed
7. clearly possible
8. unusually angry
9. suddenly popular
10. strangely sad

■ **Exercise 2** (p. 52)   **Converting adjectives to adverbs**

1. surely   6. suddenly
2. seriously   7. probably
3. √   8. exceptionally
4. easily   9. √
5. regularly   10. rapidly

■ **Exercise 4** (p. 55)   **Correcting adjective/adverb errors**

1. The mechanic who estimates the cost of repairs was . . .
2. livelier OR more lively
3. autobiographies OR autobiographical compositions
4. continuously; well
5. easily
6. √
7. reasonably exclusive residential area of Kansas City
8. √
9. worst
10. worse

5 Case

For some students, determining the case of a noun or pronoun must be like aiming at an invisible target—what they don't see they can't hit. After all, *cat* is *cat* whether it's subject of the verb, object of the preposition, or subject of the infinitive. Case matters only with pronouns—or so students would like to believe.

Now is the time to discuss the importance of inflection and syntax in signaling meaning and to make the point that as the system of inflections once present in English gradually eroded, some other way was needed to convey information about the relationship of a word to its sentence—and that way was word order.

To introduce the concept of inflection, write three words on the chalkboard: *bluckfle, rurgit, deet.* Since the words are unfamiliar ones, students are unable to guess which two are nouns and which one is a verb. Suggest that the two nouns be so marked by adding an *x*-suffix: *rurgitx* and *deetx.* Now suggest that one be marked singular (*rurgitxo*) and one plural (*deetxi*). Since in this sentence words may be ordered in any way the writer sees fit, the reader needs some system of suffixes (though prefixes could also be used) to keep the action straight. Assign a subject suffix (*deetxis*) and an object suffix (*rurgitxoj*). To review, ask students what they know about *deetxis* (noun, plural, subject) and *rurgitxoj* (noun, singular, object). Now the elements of the sentence may be arranged in various orders, but the function of the two nouns is always signaled by the suffixes:

> Bluckfle deetxis rurgitxoj.
>
> Rurgitxoj bluckfle deetxis.
>
> Deetxis rurgitxoj bluckfle.

Next add suffixes to *bluckfle* to show that it is a verb (*bluckflev*), third person plural (*bluckflevp*), and present tense (*bluckflevpe*). Now draw arrows to match the verb with the subject and write the three-word sentence in an order other than subject-verb-object to show that inflections allow syntactic flexibility. Ask students what would happen if the inflections were removed. Then use these two pairs of sentences to show the importance of word order:

1. The cat chased the mouse.
   The mouse chased the cat.
2. Margaret is leaving now.
   Is Margaret leaving now?

Readers of English depend on word order and a few inflections to tell them about the relationships between words in a sentence. Writers also use the same orders and inflections to convey information. Thus, any error in order (such as a misplaced modifier) or in inflection (case, number) confuses the meaning being signaled.

Throughout the history of English, pronouns have changed less than any other part of speech and thus retain their case forms more distinctively than nouns do. The case forms of pronouns, then, deserve study because they carry information about the way words function in a sentence, and that information helps to convey meaning. And while nouns no longer have separate forms for subjective and objective cases, they do have a possessive case.

ACTIVITIES

1. Have students bring to class a copy of an edited paragraph from a recent theme or write a paragraph for this assignment. The paragraph should include ten pronouns, five of which are personal pronouns; the copy should be neatly handwritten or typed. Ask them to exchange papers and then to underline and number all pronouns in the paragraph and on a separate sheet of paper to list in columns the pronouns, the case of each, and the reason for each case:

Pronoun	Case	Reason
a. us	objective	object of preposition
b. she	subjective	subject complement

   Students could do this activity in small groups, but guard against groups in which one student who is sure of the answers completes the exercise while everyone else looks on.

2. Ask students to collect from newspapers—campus newspapers are a readily available source—three examples of pronouns correctly used and three incorrectly used. You may wish to narrow the selection to instances of a single pronoun, a single case, or a single function.

3. Distribute copies of the campus newspaper and discuss pronouns used in that issue. If there are errors in usage, ask students to correct them, giving the appropriate rule.

4. Ask students to select the one sentence from each pair that is appropriate in formal English.

   a. It was I barbequing chicken at midnight. √
      Kim refusing to sing at the wedding rehearsal upset David and Beth.
   b. Let's you and me fly to Dallas for the weekend. √
      Could it have been them, Scott and Mike, who designed the concrete canoe?
   c. Give the message to whomever answers the telephone.
      Jerry wanted Elizabeth and me to weed the garden every day. √
   d. Professor Still is a dynamic teacher which I admire.
      The question has become who should be nominated to fill the vacancy. √

e. No one could be happier than her now that the Cubs have won three games.
That cashier is the one whom she thinks the customers voted most helpful. ✓

5. Have students write sentences to illustrate the following:

a. *we* as subject complement
b. *whoever* as subject of a clause
c. *theirs* as direct object
d. *us* as object of an infinitive
e. *her* as part of a compound appositive

6. Ask students to convert possessive nouns to possessive pronouns and possessive pronouns to possessive nouns.

a. Mark's   d. the Department of Labor's
b. theirs   e. ours
c. women's

ANSWERS TO EXERCISES

■ **Exercise 1** (p. 60)   **Choosing correct pronouns**

1. We   6. him
2. I   7. him, her
3. they   8. I, her, themselves
4. He   9. he
5. her   10. him

■ **Exercise 3** (p. 63)   **Combining sentences with *who* or *whom***

1. Hercule Poirot is a famous detective whom Agatha Christie finally kills off in *Curtain*.
2. Some parents who think they are protecting their offspring make an introvert out of an only child.
3. Does anyone remember the name of the Frenchman who built a helicopter in 1784?
4. One of the officials with whom the players had quarreled earlier called for a severe penalty.

■ **Exercise 4** (p. 63)   **Changing *who* to *whom***

1. Whom   3. whom
2. ✓   4. ✓

5. whom	8. whom
6. whom	9. [deceived] whom
7. $\checkmark$	10. whomever

■ **Exercise 5** (p. 65)   **Revising case forms**

1. who	6. $\checkmark$
2. whom, my	7. me
3. $\checkmark$	8. whom [I interviewed]
4. me	9. whom [we respect]
5. $\checkmark$	10. me

6 Agreement

The study of agreement might begin with a discussion of number and of the formation of plurals (Section **18**). Also, since agreement involves labeling nouns as third person, the term *person* might need clarification too.

Students may be troubled by the expletive *there* and by nouns— especially objects of prepositions—that intervene between subject and verb, for the two complicate agreement by obscuring the grammatical subject of a sentence. (Other inverted word orders at least hint that all may not be as it seems: *The problems of noise pollution he has studied for years. Has he studied the problems of noise pollution for years?*) Yet students do not always recognize the expletive *there* as a signal of inverted order. Instead they label it subject, and the result is a sentence like: *There's arguments for both sides.*

A second problem in identifying subjects of verbs is the students' inclination to name as subject whatever noun most closely precedes the verb and then to make the verb singular or plural according to the noun. Thus, students will write: *One of the six baskets of clean clothes were carried upstairs.* OR *Marian is the only one of those nursing majors who always finish a paper one week before it is due.* Students who make this kind of error may have forgotten the subject by the time they write the verb; or they may have mistakenly applied the rule that in a sentence with a compound subject the verb agrees with the closer one; or they may have simply not correctly identified the subject. Clarifying the use of the whichever-is-closer rule is easy enough, and having students identify and eliminate prepositional phrases as they read for subject-verb agreement will reduce their options.

Students may resist using indefinite pronouns in their writing for a number of reasons. First, they associate some of the pronouns with a degree of formality that they rarely produce (*few were turned away; each married a childhood sweetheart; either is acceptable*); they are more likely to use *few, each,* and *either* as modifiers (*few fans; each graduate; either menu*) or to choose an alternate construction (*not very many fans; the graduates; both of the menus*). Second, they are unsure about which pronouns are regularly singular and what rules govern compound subjects. Finally, students are caught between the rules of pronoun-antecedent agreement and the increasing avoidance of the generic *he, his,* or *him,* a usage that has the effect of excluding females. In such cases you can point out that English is a living, changing language; that alternatives (*his/her, his or her*) do exist; and that *their* as an alternative is becoming more acceptable even though it violates a grammatical principle.

ACTIVITIES

1. Ask students to identify the function of *there* in each of the following sentences as adverb (A) or expletive (E) and to revise expletive-*there* sentences by making singular subjects plural, plural subjects singular, and changing the verb accordingly.

   a. Near the fence there are five violets and twenty-four dandelions growing. [E]
   b. Hang the picture there to cover the smudge. [A]
   c. There stand Jennifer and Linda. [A]
   d. There happens to be a perfectly logical explanation for this chaos. [E]
   e. There seems to have been a mistake; I ordered iced tea, not ice cream. [E]

2. Ask students to make a list of collective nouns that describe groups of people and use some of those nouns in sentences. Explain that once the number is established, students should use that number consistently in the composition. Have them consult a dictionary to check current usage.

3. Ask students to collect examples of the various alternatives for handling pronoun references to such antecedents as *someone* or *a student.* Ask students which of the alternatives they prefer—

which they think will survive and why. Students might find a newspaper column or a magazine article on the subject, and you might share the suggestions and alternatives in McGraw-Hill's "Guidelines for Equal Treatment of the Sexes."

4. Have students write a paragraph comparing or contrasting two relatives, two siblings, or two friends. The paragraph should include the following elements:

   a. one expression beginning with *not to mention* or *together with*
   b. compound singular subjects both of which are preceded by *every* or *each* and joined by *and*
   c. one sentence containing expletive *there*
   d. *one* used as subject
   e. two antecedents joined by *nor*

   The elements need not follow this order, but each should be labeled appropriately.

5. Ask students to explain how context has determined the verb form in each sentence:

   a. All was forgiven when he replaced the broken window.
   b. Three of my neighbors jog daily, and all take different routes.
   c. Most were mailed out before the printing error was discovered.
   d. The argument is illogical, but none question its emotional appeal.
   e. None of the ice cream has melted.
   f. No apology was offered, and none was necessary.
   g. Half want to schedule the exam for next Tuesday.
   h. Do you think half is too few?
   i. Do any of the guides answer questions during the tour?
   j. Any who are enterprising will succeed.

6. Ask students to select the correct verb form:

   a. Not everybody (*believes,* believe) the myth of the Tooth Fairy.
   b. Phyllis is, after all, the only one who (*is,* are) gullible enough to believe that the Tooth Fairy and the Great Pumpkin are cousins.
   c. She is one of the few adults who (leaves, *leave*) cookies for the Great Pumpkin.
   d. Lately, however, she has begun to question whether either Jack Frost or leprechauns (exists, *exist*).
   e. Sitting on her mantel (*is,* are) an etching of the Statue of Liberty as well as a bowl of plastic grapes and a seashell.

ANSWERS TO EXERCISES

■ **Exercise 2** (pp. 73–74)   **Choosing correct verb forms**

1. feels
2. differ
3. was
4. adorn
5. asks
6. come
7. was
8. is
9. invade; provide
10. is

■ **Exercise 3** (p. 76)   **Choosing correct pronoun or verb forms**

1. have; their
2. needs; she
3. they
4. was; it OR were; they
5. controls; it; itself OR control; they; themselves

■ **Exercise 4** (pp. 76–77)   **Securing agreement**

1. The students . . . enjoy
2. The activities . . . seem
3. Since nearly every student eats his OR his/her OR their OR his or her
4. two of the students were
5. Everyone else was in his OR his/her OR their OR his or her
6. Two or perhaps only one . . . was
7. the inflection that indicates
8. Few . . . were
9. Everyone . . . was
10. a question that provokes

7 Verb Forms

Understanding the system of English verbs requires students to grasp an extensive network of relationships of tense to time not only in a single verb but also in sequences of verbs. For that reason, it is important for them to realize that such concepts as voice, tense, and principal parts are units of a systematic description and cannot be studied in isolation. To write *She has chosen,* for example, involves a series of interrelated choices of tense, person, number, voice, and mood.

ACTIVITIES

1. Have students write a narrative paragraph of nine to ten sentences using a variety of sentence types; all verbs must be regular, and tense forms in sequence must be logical. After several of the paragraphs have been read aloud, ask students to speculate about the future of English if all irregular verbs were outlawed (either made regular or dismissed from the language). Such an exercise shows students that some of the verbs used most frequently (such as *be, go, see*) are irregular and that eliminating irregular verbs would drastically alter English.

2. Ask students to complete these two sentences with the proper verb forms:

   a. Phil *past tense* the porcelain vase, but if Carolyn has *past participle* one, too, she won't admit it. [*bring, choose, draw, lose, steal, take*]
   b. They have *past participle* sweet corn. [*buy, can, eat, freeze, grow, raise*]

3. Ask students to review the difference between direct objects and subject complements. Then have students apply the following set of questions to the fifteen sentences below to determine whether a verb is transitive/intransitive, active/passive, linking/complete.

   a. Is the verb transitive or intransitive?
   b. If the verb is transitive, what is the direct object?
   c. If the verb is transitive, does the subject perform the action of the verb?
   d. If the verb is intransitive, is there a complement?
   e. If there is a complement, what kind is it?

   The order of these questions is designed to show that the first task—even if the ultimate one is to discover whether the verb is active or passive—is to decide whether the verb is transitive or intransitive since the answer *transitive* leads to questions *b* and *c* while the answer *intransitive* leads to questions *d* and *e*. Thus, the choices are limited so that an answer such as *transitive complete* is impossible.

   The following diagram clarifies the hierarchy of choices for students who insist on asking whether the verb is active or passive before they know whether it is transitive:

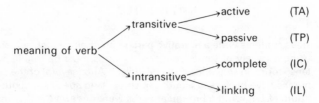

1. More hot sauce should be added to those tacos. [TP]
2. How could I have anticipated Ralph's sentence about the dead jackalope? [TA]
3. The class had been dull until yesterday. [IL]
4. I began to suspect a sense of humor upon hearing Brad identify *sea-nymph* as an exclamation. [TA]
5. Mike's days of being an outcast will cease with the end of the semester. [IC]
6. Camille went to the mountains to be alone. [IC]
7. Watching from my bedroom window, I saw her climb the tree to rescue the kitten. [TA]
8. This horse hasn't been ridden for two weeks. [TP]
9. Crystal bought a geode to add to her mineral collection. [TA]
10. Nick and Seth were applauded for their original lyrics. [TP]
11. After the moderator's long introduction, Joan began her speech on the virtues of brevity. [TA]
12. The chili con carne smelled delicious, but it was too spicy for me. [IL, IL]
13. She leaned wearily against her shopping cart. [IC]
14. Laughing uproariously at the misprint, they continued through the story. [IC]
15. Has the bill from the dentist been paid yet? [TP]

4. Verbs are classified according to their meaning as transitive or intransitive. Have students compose sentences to show the following verbs first as transitive and then as intransitive: *swim, guess, pass, govern, edge, dance.*

5. Outline passive voice by listing the features of a sentence containing a passive-voice verb:

   a. a verb consisting of a form of *to be* plus the past participle of the main verb (*were written, have been mailed*)

b. a subject which receives the action of the verb rather than one that performs the action (*The newspaper was torn. Someone tore the newspaper.*)

c. a prepositional phrase beginning with *by* and having as its object the person or thing performing the action of the verb (this prepositional phrase is sometimes optional.)

Then write the following sentences on the board and ask students to identify the features of the passive found in each:

a. Our meeting was canceled by the chairman.
b. Our meeting has been canceled by the chairman.
c. Our meeting was canceled.
d. Our meeting has been canceled.

Note: A sentence containing an indirect object as well as a direct object can also be made passive.

The judge awarded us custody.
We were awarded custody by the judge.
Custody was awarded us by the judge.

6. From students' compositions, select ten passive-voice sentences for a handout or transparency. Ask students to rewrite them, using active voice.

ANSWERS TO EXERCISES

■ **Exercise 1** (p. 85)   **Using verb forms in a pattern**

1. Yes, he gave it away.
2. You have already run a mile.
3. Yes, the man drowned.
4. They have already begun that.
5. Yes, the wind blew.
6. She has already chosen it.
7. Yes, it really happened.
8. The river has already risen.
9. Yes, you did that.
10. They have already stolen it.
11. Yes, you spun your wheels.
12. They have already frozen it.
13. Yes, he clung to that belief.

14. They have already gone to the police.
15. Yes, she knew them.
16. The fire alarm has already rung.
17. Yes, the sack burst.
18. He has already eaten it.
19. Yes, you grew these.
20. Bert has already spoken out.

■ **Exercise 2** (p. 86)   **Substituting correct forms of *sit* and *lie***

1. Jack doesn't ever want to sit down.
   Jack doesn't ever want to lie down.
2. The dog sat near the luggage.
   The dog lay near the luggage.
3. The toy soldier has been sitting in the yard.
   The toy soldier has been lying in the yard.
4. He often sits on a park bench.
   He often lies on a park bench.
5. Has it sat there all along?
   Has it lain there all along?

■ **Exercise 3** (pp. 86–87)   **Choosing correct verb forms**

1. lie	6. sitting
2. laid	7. setting
3. lain	8. sat
4. lying	9. sat
5. laid	10. sit

■ **Exercise 5** (pp. 90–91)   **Choosing correct verb forms**

1. ended	6. Having bought
2. was made	7. adjourned
3. to celebrate	8. to brand
4. to go	9. to see
5. Having finished	10. has dropped

■ **Exercise 8** (p. 93)   **Correcting verb errors**

1. ✓	6. ✓
2. gives	7. rambles
3. ✓	8. owes
4. called	9. ✓
5. to propose	10. Sit

■ **Exercise 9** (p. 94)   **Correcting verb errors**

1. If he had registered
2. If Leslie had enrolled
3. √
4. √
5. used to be
6. had entered the room . . . and began to write
7. to have a visit
8. then take the next road
9. had stolen
10. would have liked to be OR would like to have been

8   Manuscript Form

The class time devoted to explaining the requirements of manuscript form is well spent. As early in the semester as possible, describe precisely what is acceptable, provide examples of acceptable and unacceptable format, and then insist on the proper format thereafter. Otherwise, you are guaranteed sets of themes that inevitably include a few written on narrow-lined notebook paper or typed single-spaced on onionskin.

In evaluating what they have written, students should revise as well as proofread their prose. Revision refers to such changes in content as the addition of examples, the clarification of ideas, the development of unity and coherence in paragraphs (see **32h**, Reviser's Checklist); proofreading refers to changes in punctuation; spelling, and mechanics (see **8e**, Proofreader's Checklist). Both are equally essential in the preparation of a final draft. To emphasize the importance of revision, share with students the results of Nancy Sommers' study of the differences between the revision strategies of students and experienced writers in *College Composition and Communication,* December 1980, pages 378–88.

ACTIVITIES

1. Bring to class examples of legible and illegible handwriting (themes saved from previous semesters are a ready source) and

ask students for their reactions. Ask why reactions to a single example vary (the handwriting may be similar to the student's own style; the handwriting may resemble that of a person the student dislikes, etc.) and how writers could guard against negative reactions. Such comments may lead to a discussion of handwriting as an expression of a student's personality and whether students must sacrifice their handwriting style for the sake of keeping an audience.

2. Have students work in groups of three to evaluate the themes of peers. Have each essay read by two students, one using the Reviser's Checklist and one using the Proofreader's Checklist. Ask students to write in the margins any suggested corrections or revisions. Allow time for the evaluators to discuss their written comments and for the author to respond.

3. Ask students to correct proofreading errors by writing the proper form above each error; have them use a colored pencil or ink of a different color from that already used in order to facilitate checking corrections.

4. For the first few themes, ask students to chart their corrections as well as the rule for each correction. Having students include the correction symbols provides an opportunity for them to learn the marking system. **Note:** Spelling errors may be included on this chart or put on the student's list of words to study.

SAMPLE CHART

Symbol	Error (in context)	Correction	Rule
cap	studying Art	art	**9f** — Avoid unnecessary capitals.
ca	Jim going offended	Jim's	**5d** — Use the possessive case before a gerund.

ANSWERS TO EXERCISES

■ **Exercise 1** (pp. 100–01)   **Dividing words**

Words that should not be divided:

4. NATO	8. against	14. CPA	17. matches
5. gripped	13. recline	16. WFAA-FM	20. cobras

Words that may be divided, with boldface hyphens marking appropriate divisions:

1. cross-ref•er•ence	7. guess-ing	12. e•ven-tu•al
2. e•co-nom•ic	9. pres-ent	15. mag•i-cal
3. fif-teenth	10. pre-sent	18. dis-solve
6. grip-ping	11. sea-coast	19. cob-webs

9 Capitals

Capital letters, which give significance to the words they head, are a matter of convention. Students who use capitalization for emphasis, therefore, are not only ignoring conventional practices but also producing a cluttered page. The result is not significance but insignificance, for the effect of claiming importance for everything is to reduce it for anything.

Note: *A Manual of Style,* 12th ed., (University of Chicago Press, 1969) includes a detailed discussion of capitalization and abbreviations.

ACTIVITIES

1. Ask students to supply the principles of capitalization that govern the following:

   a. Jell-O; whipped cream
   b. Roman Catholic Church; catholic tastes
   c. the Great Plains; eastern South Dakota
   d. Freshman Composition; sophomores and juniors
   e. Levis; jeans

f. Lake Mead; the Allegheny and Monongahela rivers
g. Senator Nancy Kassebaum; George Bush, vice president of the United States
h. Dead Sea Scrolls; worship service
i. Korean War; the infantry
j. Canis Major; aurora borealis

2. Give students a list of titles (uncapitalized) from a set of recent themes and ask them to follow **9c** as they provide proper capitalization.

3. Ask students to write down the titles of three books and three articles they have read recently (works not related to academic requirements), and three books they would like to read as soon as they have time.

4. Bring a telephone directory to class to illustrate conventions regarding names in the yellow pages.

ANSWERS TO EXERCISE

■ **Exercise 2** (p. 114)   **Supplying capitals**

1. English; I; Thanksgiving; U.S. Constitution
2. West; Carlsbad Caverns; Yellowstone National Park; Painted Desert; Rockies; Pacific Ocean
3. God's; Bible; We; Democrats; Senator Attebury
4. Robert Sherrill's; *The Saturday Night Special* [*and*] *Other Guns* [*with*] *Which Americans Won* [*the*] *West, Protected Bootleg Franchises, Slew Wildlife, Robbed Countless Banks, Shot Husbands Purposely* [*and by*] *Mistake,* [*and*] *Killed Presidents—Together* [*with the*] *Debate* [*over*] *Continuing Same*

10 Italics

Students who rely on italics to emphasize special meaning have yet to learn that an effective sentence emphasizes certain ideas by its diction and word arrangement and that every part contributes to both meaning and arrangement or structure. Just as the architect selects the type of exterior finish appropriate to the style of the house, so the students must choose elements of mechanics and punctuation appropriate to the meaning and the arrangement of the words.

If, however, you suggest that students try ways other than italics to emphasize ideas but do not specify those ways, students usually opt for quotation marks or (infrequently) capitalization. As a rule, these choices are equally ineffective because the problem lies with the choice of words, not with the choice of marks for emphasis (see also **16d**). Instead, students should work to master substitution (for single words) and arrangement (for relative importance of ideas). Thus, the sentence *His laugh* was *"funny"* might become *His laugh was a burst of throaty gasps* or *With a burst of throaty gasps he laughed.*

The use of italics to identify a word used as a word sometimes confuses students because they tend to see words as individual items listed in dictionaries or vocabulary exercises or as units in a sentence; they can therefore have difficulty imagining a sentence in which a word is used as such. Examples using proper names clarify the rule: *Katherine and Catharine are variations of Catherine* (compare with: *Catherine addressed the envelope*). A useful rule of thumb is that if a word can be preceded by *the word,* it should be italicized (*The word philology means "love of words"; the discipline of philology is the study of language development*).

ACTIVITIES

1. Ask students to list the titles of their favorites: three books, three magazines, three films, three television programs, three songs. Ask students to list the titles of two textbooks they are using in other courses and the titles of two chapters from each; the titles of two journals in their major field (such as *English Journal*) and the titles of two articles from recent issues of each. Ask them to list the title of the last play or film they attended on campus and the title they would give their autobiography.

2. Have students identify which item in each of the pairs is correct:

   a. *60 Minutes* √   "Consumer Reports"
   b. *Chicago Tribune* √   Oh, Susanna
   c. *U.S.S. Jackson*   Hamlet √
   d. the *Bible*   "The Lottery" √
   e. *Gone With The Wind* √   "Ordinary People"

ANSWERS TO EXERCISE

■ **Exercise** (pp. 118–19) **Underlining words that should be italicized**

1. *U.S. News & World Report*
2. *Queen Mary; The Divine Comedy*
3. *d; t;* partner; pretty
4. *The Magic Flute; très magnifique*
5. *Battle of the Centaurs; Madonna of the Steps*

11 Abbreviations and Numbers

The emphasis in **11a-11d** is on spelling out words, for formal prose does not yet admit all of the convenient abbreviations students would like to use to reduce the time spent writing. Certain inappropriate abbreviations appear more frequently than others—the titles *Prof.* and *Sen.*, names of states, days, and months. Yet the writer's convenience is less important than the reader's needs. Abbreviation-laden writing channels the reader's attention away from the message and toward the symbols to be decoded, thus interfering with the process of communication.

The common Latin expressions (*e.g., i.e., et al., etc.*) deserve comment not so much because students use them in their writing as because they encounter them in their reading. Often unfamiliar with both the abbreviation and its Latin phrase, students ignore valuable information because they don't know how to interpret its relationship to the sentence they are reading. Further, they misspell such abbreviations as *etc.* (as *ect.* or *and etc.*) or *vs.* (as *vrs.*) because they have had little experience with them.

The question of when to spell out numbers is one that students always ask. Although **11e** specifies that numbers of one or two words be written out, students often think that the numbers one through ten (or sometimes one through twenty) are spelled out while figures are used for all other numbers. Perhaps they cannot distinguish numbers in series and statistics from numbers in other usage (see "Special Usage Regarding Numbers," number 7).

The use of *from* and *to* with dates also requires comment. Students who have developed their own abbreviations for note-taking (*in 1981–82, from 1981–82,* or *fm 81–82*) may be unaware of the distinction between *from 1981 to 1983* and *in 1981–82—from* and *to* are used together, or the hyphen is used without *from;* but *from* and the hyphen are not used together.

ACTIVITIES

1. Discuss the need for clarity when using acronyms, referring to the grammatical glossary and to Section **27** on establishing a point of reference. Ask students to write a sentence using an acronym that readers are likely to be unfamiliar with.

2. Have students write sentences telling:
   a. the month, date, year, city, and state of their birth
   b. their school address; their home address
   c. the number of seniors in their high-school graduating class
   d. the dates of employment for a recent job, preferably one at which they no longer work
   e. the ideal salary offered them upon graduation and the ideal location of that job

3. Ask students to write sentences about three or four statistics found in an almanac or in *The Guinness Book of Records.*

ANSWERS TO EXERCISES

■ **Exercise 1** (p. 123) **Striking out forms inappropriate in formal writing**

Inappropriate *forms which students should strike out are listed below.*

1. a dr.
2. in the U.S.
3. in Calif. and Ill.
4. on Magnolia St.
5. Charleston, S.C.
7. on Aug. 15
8. for Jr.
10. before six in the A.M.

■ **Exercise 2** (p. 126) **Using appropriate shortened forms**

1. on June 15 OR on June 15th
2. Dr. Ernest Threadgill OR Ernest Threadgill, M.D.
3. $30 million OR $30,000,000

4. Janine Keith, C.P.A.
5. the UN OR the U.N.
6. 1 P.M. OR 1 p.m. OR 1:00 P.M. OR 1:00 p.m.
7. by December 1, 1985 OR by 1 December 1985
8. at the bottom of page 15
9. the USN OR the U.S.N. OR the U.S. Navy
10. 400 B.C.
11. in act 1, scene 2 OR Act I, Scene 2
12. (1985–1990) OR (1985–90)

12 The Comma

To use commas conscientiously is to keep in mind the structure and the readability of the sentence. Effective writers place commas in order to separate and clarify elements of the sentence in accord with the patterns of English, thereby giving perspective to and showing relationships between the parts of the sentence. Effective writers know that knowledge of sentence structure and the ability to use commas correctly go together; they also know that the pauses signaled by commas should facilitate the reader's comprehension of ideas.

Commas separate elements, thus grouping and isolating on all levels: the level of word (*aggressive, articulate salesperson*), of phrase (*Janet's favorite pet, an Irish setter, requires frequent grooming*), and of clause (*She loves to read biographies of artists, but her favorite summer pastime is attending craft shows*). Commas even separate one level from another; for example, a sentence modifier is separated from the sentence by a comma (*Unfortunately, the class was canceled before we could register for it*). Because commas work within as well as between levels, it is useful to point out the difficulty in reading a sentence with too many—albeit correctly placed—commas:

> When Jean, humming and smiling mysteriously, entered the crowded, hushed waiting room, she saw two sullen children, a distraught parent, and a harried receptionist, who was retrieving scattered toys.

In this sentence the number of ideas obscures the major divisions of adverb clause and main clause. The commas do not cause the problem; they are an indication of it.

To help students see the problem, ask them for revisions to improve the readability of the sentence. Allow them to see that some rearrangements change the meaning. Although creating two sentences is one option, assure them that as long as the two major divisions are clearly marked, all of the ideas can remain in one sentence:

> Jean, humming and smiling mysteriously, entered the crowded, hushed waiting room; there she saw two sullen children, a distraught parent, and a harried receptionist, who was retrieving scattered toys.

Two tests help students identify coordinate adjectives. First, coordinate adjectives may be joined by *and:*

soggy, bedraggled puppy	OR	soggy and bedraggled puppy
	BUT NOT	
difficult biology exam		difficult and biology exam
crumpled typing paper		crumpled and typing paper

Second, coordinate adjectives may be reversed and still communicate the same meaning:

soggy, bedraggled puppy	OR	bedraggled, soggy puppy
	BUT NOT	
difficult biology exam		biology difficult exam
crumpled typing paper		typing crumpled paper
long wooden ladder		wooden long ladder

ACTIVITIES

1. Ask students to insert commas between main clauses separated by a coordinating conjunction:

   a. We raked the leaves into ten small piles but Jerry argued that three large piles would look better.
   b. I fertilized the garden and watered it thoroughly every week.
   c. Did you buy carpet for the kitchen floor or did you decide to wait until parquet flooring is on sale before you remodel the kitchen?
   d. They saved their money for a two-week vacation in New York but finally decided to rent a houseboat instead.
   e. Marlene did not want to wax her car nor did she want to pay someone else to do it.

2. Have students write sentences following the pattern *Adverb clause, main clause.* Then have students rewrite the sentences

using the pattern *Main clause adverb clause.* Suggest as subordinators *as soon as, because, until, wherever,* and *provided;* or have students select from those listed in **12b**.

3. Ask students to create a dialogue between two personalities who ordinarily would have little opportunity to talk together. Pairings might include Ralph Nader and Bobby Unser, Marabel Morgan and Dolly Parton, J. R. Ewing and F. Lee Bailey, Hawkeye Pierce and Henry David Thoreau, Erma Bombeck and Ann Landers. Students should use each of the punctuation patterns shown in Note 2, page 143.

4. To help students distinguish restrictive from nonrestrictive clauses, have them answer each of the following questions twice in complete sentences; the first with a restrictive clause, the second with a nonrestrictive clause.

   a. Who has helped you the most?

      1. An instructor who explains rules clearly helps me become a better writer.
      2. Professor Grimes, who always returns papers promptly, advised me to use subordination more often.

   b. Who listens to your problems?
   c. What job would you like upon graduation?
   d. Which sibling do you most often compete with?
   e. Who is one person you admire?

5. Before assigning Section **12**, have students select one body paragraph from a recent theme, copy every comma use, and give a reason for it. Suggest that students use a chart and that they be honest in listing their reasons:

Comma	Reason
went downstairs, he	comma after an introductory clause
claque, cleek, or *clique*	comma with items in a series
For example,	don't know; sounded good

Students' reasons may range from an honest "don't know" to the statement of a rule. When students have finished, collect the chart and the paragraph. After Section **12** has been taught, return the chart and the paragraph, asking students to correct the punctuation and then to make a justification chart for the revised paragraph. Have students compare the two charts and write a brief description of how their use of the comma has improved.

6. Ask students to explain the uses of the comma in one paragraph taken from one of their textbooks or a favorite magazine.

ANSWERS TO EXERCISES

Since punctuation is often a matter of individual preference, much of the key to exercises in Sections **12–17** should be considered as merely suggestive—indicative of one instructor's preferences.

■ **Exercise 1** (p. 131)   **Linking sentences with *and, but, or, nor, for, so,* or *yet***

1. strikes, *and* another [OR *so* OR *and so*]
2. bars, *nor* did it make
3. immediately, *or* they may
4. vacation, *for* they needed
5. whistle, *but* she cannot

■ **Exercise 2** (pp. 131–32)   **Inserting commas before connectives**

1. questionnaires, and they had
2. fill, for Bob
3. later, but I
4. movie, and the
5. party, but Gary

■ **Exercise 3** (pp. 134–35)   **Identifying and punctuating introductory clauses or phrases**

The first and last words of the main clauses are given in italics. Introductory elements are identified, and the punctuation is justified within brackets, in accordance with rule **12b**. Different answers, however, may be justified as an exception to **12b** (in accordance with text page 133) or on the basis of intonation indicating a nonparenthetical element.

1. days, *you . . . displayed* [adverb clause]
2. *example, you . . . Anything* [phrase]
3. opinion *their . . . yourself* [phrase]
4. sledgehammer, *these . . . desires* [phrase]
7. do, *buy . . . it* [adverb clause]
8. hours, *you . . . way* [phrase]

■ **Exercise 5** (pp. 139–40)   **Using commas with nonrestrictive elements**

1. √
2. √
3. hometown, which . . . heard of.
4. √
5. Thompson, sitting . . . window.
6. √
7. Venice, which . . . next.
8. √
9. Smith, who . . . bank.
10. √

■ **Exercise 6** (pp. 141–42)   **Combining sentences and inserting commas**

1. The General Sherman Tree, a giant sequoia in California, is about 270 feet tall.
2. Those are pill bugs, not insects.
3. On April 1, 1980, his divorced wife married his lawyer, Bill Wynne.
4. The publisher's address is 757 Third Avenue, New York, New York 10017, not 757 Madison Avenue.
5. We moved to Taos, New Mexico, one of the popular sun states, on 30 September 1978.

■ **Exercise 7** (p. 144)   **Explaining correctly used commas**

2. True, we—**12d** [Comparable to introductory *Yes*—see **12b(3)**]
3. However, the treaty—**12d** OR **12b(3)**
   destruction,'' and—**12a**
   bodies, it—**12b**
4. case, the—**12d** OR variation of **12b**
   treaty, all by itself, is—**12d**
   ones, the bullies, the maniacs, the suicidal types, OR—**12c**
   ''progress,'' ''liberation,'' OR—**12c**

5. colony, as well as the Earth itself, would — **12d**
6. today, we — **12b** OR **12d**
7. system, life — **12b**
   Normans, Berbers — **12c**

■ **Exercise 8** (pp. 144–46)   **Inserting needed commas**

1. drunkenness, nor
2. *Hazel, Beverly, Marian, Frances,* and *Shirley*
3. floors, far . . . earth, were
4. change, the alteration
   spoken, not the written, form
5. said, "Look, Chief, you. . . ."
6. Incidentally, supporting
   expensive, some
7. polite, almost dainty
   applause, the kind
8. believe, women
9. breathes, in
10. month, the time of murder, robbery, assault, suicide, and Christ-mas
11. much, eh, Doctor
12. spring, a brilliant
    September 22, 1979, in the
13. Detroit, weather
14. witless, ugly, brutal, insensate, stupid
15. understands, Alaska
16. moonlight, the hot
17. categorized, no matter
18. lived," said Mick Pattemore, his accent
    Sweetwater, Texas, but Somerset, England
19. sports, it
20. relationship, smooth

■ **Exercise 9** (p. 146)   **Class discussion of commas**

In sentence 3 commas could be inserted as follows:

    you, you   [**12b**]
    realized, and   [**12a**]
    it, the whole   [**12b**]
    lash up, squirming   [**12d**]

In the closing sentence the third part of rule **12d** *can explain the parenthetical or appended elements.*

13 Superfluous Commas

Once students have studied the rules in Section **12**, the result—usually for the next theme or two—is commas, commas everywhere. Even students who had no problems with the comma before tend to over-comma their prose until they can comfortably and correctly apply the rules that their style most often calls upon. By reemphasizing the comma's relationship to structure and readability, however, you can stem this flow.

Short introductory phrases and slightly parenthetical phrases (**13c**) become the objects of students' desire to separate elements. Introductory prepositional phrases are especially likely to be set off by commas if they contain more than three words (*In modern research laboratories*).

Also, students try to improve readability by using a comma between the subject and verb in the belief that the comma helps the reader see the most important separation in the sentence. What they do not realize is that while English sentences are binary, the separation of subject and verb by a comma works against the completion of meaning, for once readers come upon the subject or the verb, they then search out the word(s) that complete the central thought.

ACTIVITIES

1. Ask students who make the errors discussed in Section **13** to complete a justification chart after they have made the necessary corrections in their themes.

2. Have students correct the misused commas in the following sentences. (See **13b**.)

   a. Beth makes lists of things to do, and plans her time efficiently.
   b. The most important tasks are at the top of the list, so, she concentrates on them first.
   c. Beth has learned to accomplish even more by delegating household chores to her children yet, she always reserves some time every evening for her hobbies.
   d. Playing backgammon, or cross-country skiing are her winter favorites, but, during the summer she prefers racing hot-air balloons.

ANSWERS TO EXERCISES

■ **Exercise 1** (p. 149)   **Explaining the absence of commas**

1. **13c**   3. **13b**   5. **13c**   7. **13b**
2. **13a**   4. **13d**   6. **13b; 13c**

■ **Exercise 2** (pp. 149–50)   **Changing sentences and deleting unneeded commas**

1. trees and pounded
2. facts and predicts
3. work and may
4. People who lead rather than demand often get good results.
5. A boy who is willing to work can get a job here.

■ **Exercise 3** (p. 150)   **Circling superfluous commas**

1. are⊙ at least⊙ three
2. First⊙ is
3. favorite⊙ fishing
   spot⊙ where
4. fish⊙ is
   he⊙ generally⊙ gets
5. person⊙ who
6. him⊙ and
   anything⊙ fit
   as⊙ perch
7. bank⊙ by
8. one⊙ great
   big⊙ wad
   out⊙ and
   pole⊙ so
9. Then⊙ he
10. He⊙ sometimes⊙ dozes.
11. Also⊙ he
12. CORRECT
13. CORRECT
14. line⊙ and⊙ to

14   The Semicolon

Like the comma, the semicolon clarifies the structure of the sentence and thus increases readability. And as with the comma, the correct use of the semicolon depends on students' mastery of sentence structure. Hence, beginning the study of the semicolon with a discussion of the phrase "parts of unequal grammatical rank" facilitates the study of this section and offers an opportunity to review phrases and clauses.

Levels of grammatical rank may be classified according to their ability to function as an independent unit of expression; from highest to lowest, the levels are sentence, main clause, subordinate clause, phrase (noun, verb, prepositional, gerund, infinitive, participial), word, and letter. Both a sentence and a main clause may function as independent units; however, a sentence ranks above a main clause because a sentence may include a number of main clauses (*They lived in Minneapolis until they retired; then they moved to Santa Barbara.*).

A semicolon separates parts of equal grammatical rank but not parts from two different ranks. It may, for example, separate two sentences or two clauses or a series of identical structures already containing commas. It does not, however, separate different types of phrases from each other, such as a noun phrase from a verb phrase or a participial phrase from a noun phrase.

ACTIVITIES

1. Review phrases and clauses by asking students to label each of the following P or C:

   a. without losing his sense of humor   [P]
   b. after he had brushed the pie from his lap   [C]
   c. until someone apologized   [C]
   d. because of the unfortunate accident   [P]
   e. while they were carrying full trays   [C]

2. Review main and subordinate clauses by asking students to label the clauses in the following sentences (subordinate clauses are bracketed):

   a. We know [who planted the two plastic flamingos in our yard.]
   b. [Although we still have them,] they are now in a dark corner of the basement.

   c. Emily and Grant, [who collect barbed wire,] think [everyone should collect something.]

   d. Now we have a flamingo puppet and flamingo salt and pepper shakers to add to the lawn ornaments.

   e. I wonder [if there is a club for people (who collect flamingo curios.)]

3. Ask students to tell whether or not the units in each item are of equal grammatical rank and to what rank each unit belongs:

   a. As soon as she spoke / because of her wit   [clause / phrase]

   b. She spoke with authority / when she delivered her speech [sentence or main clause / subordinate clause]

   c. Phrasing her thoughts carefully / she measured the crowd's reaction while she spoke   [phrase / sentence]

   d. An articulate and calm speaker / a speaker of unsurpassed poise   [phrase / phrase]

   e. She spoke; they listened / she spoke while they listened [sentence / sentence]

   f. Should have been listening attentively / as she replied [phrase / clause]

   g. Offering the latest statistics, she refuted the argument that he gave / to have refuted it so effortlessly   [sentence / phrase]

   h. Since the proposal was defeated / her rational argument was accepted by even those who had been opposed at first [clause / sentence]

   i. According to the latest statistics / against the proposal [phrase / phrase]

   j. She knew she had won / she congratulated herself [sentence / sentence or main clause]

4. Ask students to write two sentences for each pattern, punctuating the sentences as in the pattern.

   a. Subordinate clause, main clause; main clause subordinate clause.

   b. Main clause; transitional phrase, main clause.

   c. Main clause; main clause.

   d. Participial phrase, main clause subordinate clause; main clause.

   e. Main clause with items in a series; conjunctive adverb, main clause subordinate clause.

5. Have students collect five sentences containing semicolons and identify the rule for each use. Encourage students to locate sentences for both **14a** and **14b**. Ask students what they conclude about the use of semicolons, such as how often they are found; whether they more often illustrate rule **14a** or **14b**; and whether they are found more often in informal or formal writing.

6. Reinforce rule **14a** and relate it to use of the period (**17a**) by dictating pairs of ideas that could be written as one compound sentence or as two simple sentences. Ask students to decide which is better, after referring to **23a**.

ANSWERS TO EXERCISES

■ **Exercise 1** (p. 154)   **Using semicolons between main clauses**

1. The scientists did not accept this theory; they did not ridicule it.
2. Popular TV comedy series occasionally have spinoffs; for instance, from *The Mary Tyler Moore Show* there came *Rhoda, Lou Grant,* and *Too Close for Comfort.*
3. He took a course in the art of self-defense; later, during a class demonstration, he broke his wrist.
4. Tony himself cut and polished the turquoise; it is a beauty.
5. The team kept on losing; as a result, the morale of the whole school was low.

■ **Exercise 2** (p. 155)   **Using semicolons to separate items in a series**

1. On the talk show were three guests: T. J. Ott, a psychic; Charles Shelton, a local ufologist; and Abbish Ludah, a guru.
2. We sold everything at our benefit flea market: many dishes and vases, old and cracked; fishing gear; garden tools; and half-used tubes of lipstick.

■ **Exercise 3** (pp. 156–57)   **Correcting misused semicolons**

1. afternoon, never
2. bore, at least
3. peeves, jokes OR peeves: jokes OR peeves —jokes
4. mechanic, her OR mechanic: her OR mechanic —her
5. charge, the OR charge —the

■ **Exercise 5** (pp. 157–58)   **Using commas and semicolons**

Optional commas are enclosed in parentheses.

1. 1980s(,) for
2. Felipe, a visiting professor from Kenya, says
3. fish, . . . rhubarb, . . . tomatoes, and
4. scrawny, mangy-looking
5. firewood, I began
6. his wife, Jerry
7. Still(,) in high school(,) we . . . facts(,) such as 1066, the Battle of Hastings; 1914–1918, World War I; 1939–1945, World War II; and 1969, the first
8. Rockies; to tell the truth, however, they
9. mercy; his victim(,) for justice
10. end; however, my

15   The Apostrophe

Of the three uses of the apostrophe, the possessive case of nouns and indefinite pronouns causes students the most trouble. First they must recognize the situations that require the possessive and then work out a method for affixing its sign. Since the possessive case signals more than ownership alone, students may not recognize all of the occasions that call for it. In *An Introductory English Grammar,* 2nd ed., (Holt, 1971, pages 127–28), Norman C. Stageberg lists six relationships that are signaled (the examples here are similar to those Stageberg uses):

possession	David's videorecorder
description or characterization	driver's license
origin	Dillard's prose
measure—time	a day's time
—value	two cents' worth
—space	at arm's length
subject of act	Steve's regret; he regrets
object of act	Mary Ann's captors; someone captured her

But knowing when to use the possessive does not guarantee knowing how to use it. Many a student has avoided deciding 's or s' by writing the apostrophe above the s, thus suggesting that in the haste of getting down the idea the student intended the correct placement but failed (and students smile knowingly when the instructor says that this subterfuge is not unfamiliar). Students can follow a three-step process to select the correct form. First, they decide the word; second, they decide the number; third, they decide the sign of possession, as in these examples:

dean	(sing.) dean	**15a(1)** dean's
woman	(pl.) women	**15a(2)** women's
Richards	(pl.) Richardses	**15a(2)** Richardses'
sheep	(sing.) sheep	**15a(2)** sheep's
Secretary of State	(pl.) Secretaries of State	**15a(3)** Secretaries of State's

Thus, rather than confronting number and possession simultaneously, students learn to determine number first and spell plurals correctly before affixing the sign of possession.

Finally, knowing how to use possessive forms requires students to distinguish between personal and indefinite pronouns, for indefinite pronouns take 's but personal pronouns do not. After all, they may think, a pronoun is a pronoun and possessive is possessive, so the possessive forms of *anybody* and *it* are *anybody's* and *it's*. A review of indefinite and personal pronouns may be necessary, or if the only troublesome form is *its,* then distinguishing between the possessive and the contraction may be sufficient; in fact, you may wish simply to point out that *its* corresponds in form to *hers* and *his.*

ACTIVITIES

1. If necessary, have students review **18e** (forming the plural of nouns). Then ask them to write the singular and plural possessive forms for each of the following:

chemist	chemist's	chemists'
class	class's OR class' (depending on context)	classes'
committee	committee's	committees'
Elk City	Elk City's	Elk Citys'
fox	fox's	foxes'
beach	beach's	beaches'
staff	staff's	staffs' OR staves'
volcano	volcano's	volcano(e)s'
cactus	cactus's OR cactus'	cacti's OR cactuses'

member-at-large	member-at-large's	members-at-large's
people	people's	peoples'
other	other's	others'

Ask students for which, if any, they would use *of* instead of *'s* (such as the votes of the two members-at-large or the ceremony honoring the mayors of the two Elk Citys). Also single out *each other* and *one another* for discussion: although plural in meaning, the possessive forms are *each others'* and *one another's*. Ask the class to distinguish differences in meaning shown by *other's, others'*, and *others*.

2. Have students supply the two forms that correspond to the one already supplied, rewording as necessary.

     EXAMPLE: It is <u>Nancy's</u> gift; her gift; hers.

     a. It is _____ car (*their*).
     b. I ordered _____ dinners (*Ethan's and my*).
     c. This racquet belongs to _____ (*you*).
     d. The camper is _____ (*his*).
     e. _____ favorite color is yellow (*Frances's*).

3. Have students write these sentences as they are being dictated.

     I wonder whose essay was typed on graph paper. Whether it's hers or his makes no difference. This paper with its fine lines makes reading difficult. Who's going to argue that it's acceptable manuscript form?

ANSWERS TO EXERCISES

■ **Exercise 1** (p. 161)   **Using apostrophes to indicate the possessive case**

1. Johnny's tape decks
2. the Weinsteins' boat
3. Bess's (OR Bess') and Mary's voices
4. the editor-in-chief's efforts
5. Doris's (OR Doris') strategy
6. a quarter's worth
7. somebody else's ideas
8. Dickens' stories OR Dickens's stories
9. women's shoes
10. Henry and Ross' song OR Henry and Ross's song
    OR Henry's and Ross' song OR Henry's and Ross's song

■ **Exercise 2** (p. 163)   **Using apostrophes correctly**

1. students' (Option: 1970's)
2. CORRECT
3. Ross's
4. They're
5. '84; Jerry's
6. It's; C.P.A.'s; isn't
7. CORRECT
8. *e*'s; *d*'s; Hildegarde's; *u*'s
9. else's
10. Granddad's; Everybody's; nobody's
11. It's an
12. There's

16 Quotation Marks

Sections **16a, b,** and **e** contain information students will use as they write their research papers. For that reason, this section (along with **17i** on the ellipsis mark) can be logically included in the part of the course devoted to the research paper. Emphasis should be placed on accurate quotation as well as accurate punctuation since the respect given a piece of writing is at least in part a result of its author's respect for others' material.

As students look at a passage, they should ask: What is the controlling idea of this passage? Is the controlling idea related to the thesis of my paper? If so, exactly how? What point does it support or illustrate? What are the two or three key phrases? Do the phrases merit direct quotation, or could the key ideas be as effective if they were paraphrased? Students who learn how to evaluate sources in this fashion are more easily convinced that other sources should support their ideas, not replace them; writers who have something they think worth saying will not want too many or overly long quotations robbing them of that opportunity. At the same time, they do not risk losing their reader's patience (students often admit that as soon as they see a long prose quotation, they decide not to read it).

The following example shows the successive embedding indicated by the alternation of double and single quotation marks:

Original source:
Few can read Mark Bradley's "Chronicles of a 'Suburban Rookie' at the Annual Block Party" without giggling, chortling, or roaring at the essayist's collection of neighborhood types.

—Elizabeth Cooke

Sentence in a Research Paper:
Reader's of Bradley's essay can hardly think of suburbanites as dull; according to Elizabeth Cooke, "few can read 'Chronicles of a

"Suburban Rookie'' at the Annual Block Party' without giggling, chortling, or roaring at the essayist's collection of neighborhood types.''

Although students rarely need all three levels, they should know that a method exists for handling the situation when it arises.

A more common problem is the overuse of quotation marks for slang or colloquial words. In an attempt to demonstrate their recognition that the word does not fit the rest of the prose, students add quotation marks rather than revise. Believing they have signaled a special meaning, they have in fact apologized for weakness. Attempts at irony, humor or cleverness deserve attention. Students may have little awareness of irony, and still less experience conveying it in writing, so they will benefit from your analysis of the reasons for the misused quotation marks and some suggestions for more effective ways to convey ideas.

ACTIVITIES

1. Ask students to identify direct and indirect quotations and to punctuate the sentences.

   a. She wondered why she had agreed to babysit the twins
   b. Have I forgotten what they did the last time she mused
   c. Well she sighed at least they can't have any more mining expeditions in the backyard their shovels mysteriously disappeared
   d. She had forgotten to ask whether their batons had also been confiscated since her last visit
   e. Perhaps I just don't remember she declared how mischievous two little girls can be

2. Ask students to gather five sentences on a topic of their choice (language, marriage, heroes, success, philosophy, etc.). Then have them write sentences that quote the passages they have collected and ask them to provide documentation.

3. Ask students to write down an actual conversation. To concentrate on recording what is said, the students should not take part in the conversation; an overheard conversation or some radio or television dialogue works well. Once the dialogue is on paper, the students should add appropriate punctuation marks and dialogue tags.

4. Using an essay to which all students have access, write a series of quotations which students are to check for accuracy. Include an

error in spelling, an omitted word, an omitted single quotation mark, omitted double quotation marks, transposed words, improper capitalization, etc. Select different sentences for each error, and include two or three accurate sentences in the exercise.

5. Ask students to follow **16a(1)** or **(2)** as they quote one passage of prose or poetry that appeals to them.

ANSWERS TO EXERCISES

■ **Exercise 1** (pp. 168–69)   **Punctuating direct and indirect quotations**

Sentences containing indirect quotations may vary somewhat. Tense may vary in direct quotations.

1. Doris said, "I have a theory about you."
2. Allen announced, "I have read 'The Sunless Sea.'"
3. A Weight Watcher, Eileen explained, "I can eat as much as I want—of vegetables like spinach, eggplant, and zucchini."
4. Clyde asked whether I would go to the opera with him.
5. Last night Pruett said, "I think that Amanda's favorite quotation is 'Tomorrow belongs to me.'"

■ **Exercise 2** (p. 170)   **Using quotation marks correctly**

1. "2001,"
2. "stoked" means "fantastically happy on a surfboard." (Option: italics instead of quotation marks)
3. "A Circle in the Fire."
4. "Sighting the Target."
5. "Thomas Jefferson once said, 'Never spend your money before you have it.'"

■ **Exercise 3** (p. 172)   **Inserting needed quotation marks**

1. "Those Were the Days."
2. "Get aholt," instead of "get ahold,"
3. "No," Peg said, "I didn't . . . bananas yet!"
4. "Loveliest of Trees."
5. "Why . . . milk?" my grandmother used to ask. "Be glad . . . to spill."
6. "As for me," Socrates said, "all I . . . nothing."
7. "Isn't travel . . . self-search?"

8. "The Old Folks"
9. "The Star-Spangled Banner"?
10. Catherine said, "Do the townspeople ever say to me 'You're a born leader'? Yes, lots of times, and when they do, I just tell them my motto is 'Lead, follow, or get the heck out of the way'!'" OR . . . out of the way!'"

17   The Period and Other Marks

The literal meaning of *punctuate* is ''to mark with a point.'' Inexperienced writers, faced with a number of marks to signal intonation patterns and the relative importance of ideas within sentences, may simply ignore them, preferring to use the dash for all internal punctuation and the period for the end of every sentence. Experienced writers, however, understand that observing the proprieties of punctuation enables them to communicate more effectively than relying on one or two marks to make all the distinctions of nine.

Punctuation exercises and activities give students not only practice with individual marks but also awareness of the options and distinctions available for a single instance. As a result, they learn that they can communicate meaning through punctuation as well as through diction and word arrangement.

ACTIVITIES

1. Ask students to write sentences with the following information, first using a colon and then a dash. Example: *Three famous women who never married are Elizabeth Blackwell, Maria Montessori, and Emily Dickinson.* (*Book of Lists,* p. 278)

> Marriage is not a prerequisite of success: the careers of Elizabeth Blackwell, Maria Montessori, and Emily Dickinson show that a woman is not successful in her job because she is married.

> Elizabeth Blackwell, Maria Montessori, Emily Dickinson—these are famous women who never married.

a. The three most landed-on spaces in Monopoly are Illinois Avenue, Go, and B. & O. Railroad (*Book of Lists,* p. 375).

    b. Three benefits of regular exercise are improved body tone, increased endurance, and increased self-respect.

    c. Three words beginning with *dh* are *dhak, dharma,* and *dhole.*

    d. Three famous American writers who married are Nathaniel Hawthorne, F. Scott Fitzgerald, and Robert Frost.

    e. Three U.S. Presidents whose birthdays occur in March are Andrew Jackson, John Tyler, and Grover Cleveland.

    f. Nicknames for *Mary* are *Mamie, May, Molly,* and *Polly.*

2. Have students compose sentences to illustrate each of the following:
   a. a direct question
   b. an indirect question
   c. a double direct question
   d. a direct quotation containing an indirect question
   e. question marks between parts of a series

3. *Parentheses* comes from the Greek *parentithenai,* meaning ''a putting in beside,'' and this exactly describes the act of interpolating material that is independent from the syntax of the sentence but that qualifies the ideas in it. Parenthetical information is apart from yet related to. A writer must decide how much emphasis the parenthetical information should receive and then use the corresponding punctuation mark. Dashes emphasize most strongly, parentheses less so, and commas (because they are the commonest of the three) least. Have students discuss the effect of the punctuation in each sentence:

   a. No one—not even his mother—recognized him after he had lost seventy pounds.
   b. No one (not even his mother) recognized him after he had lost seventy pounds.
   c. No one, not even his mother, recognized him after he had lost seventy pounds.

   Ask them how the punctuation marks in each sentence reflect the writer's attitude toward the weight loss and other people's reaction to it.

4. Lists enumerated within a sentence are separated by commas and the numbers are enclosed in parentheses. Lists in vertical columns use numbers followed by a period:

   > In deciding whether to quote from a source, a writer considers (1) the authority of the writer, (2) the relationship of the

passage to the thesis of the research paper, and (3) the function of the passage in the research paper.

In deciding whether to quote from a source, a writer considers:

1. the authority of the writer
2. the relationship of the passage to the thesis of the research paper
3. the function of the passage in the research paper.

Have students enumerate the courses required for their major field of study, the arguments for a career in their major field of study, the arguments against a career in that field, and five questions to ask when considering a career in that field.

5. Following the structure of Exercise 5, use passages from several related articles (perhaps those in the students' anthology of essays) and ask students to quote according to instructions. Or use one passage reproduced on an overhead transparency and highlight the words to be omitted. Ask students to write a direct quotation omitting the words you specify.

6. Ask students to collect examples of sentences punctuated according to **17a** (three illustrations required here), **17e** (three illustrations), **17f** (two illustrations), and **17i** (two illustrations). Or ask for one example for each of the four sections.

7. Have students use the punctuation marks in this chapter as they revise one or two paragraphs from their themes. Then ask them to select what they think are three major punctuation revisions and explain what was gained by each.

ANSWERS TO EXERCISES

■ **Exercise 2** (p. 179)   **Adding colons**

1. 12**:**30; quotation**:**
2. √
3. safe**:**
4. periodicals**:**
5. √

■ **Exercise 3** (p. 179) **Using semicolons or colons between main clauses**

1. purpose:
2. purpose;
3. certain;
4. certain:

■ **Exercise 4** (pp. 184–85) **Punctuating parenthetical elements**

Punctuation setting off parenthetical matter may vary.

1. Gibbs—or is it his twin brother?—plays
2. Joseph, who is Gordon's brother, is
3. "I admit that I—" he began
4. everything—more
5. courses—for example, French and biology—demand
6. Silverheels (1918–1980) played
7. fool [sic] the
8. *zipper,* once a trademark like Polaroid, is
9. lakes—these
10. innovations—for example, the pass / fail system—did not

■ **Exercise 5** (p. 187) **Using the ellipsis mark**

According to John Donne, "No man is an island . . . every man is a piece of the continent, a part of the main. . . . Any man's death diminishes me because I am involved in mankind."

■ **Exercise 6** (pp. 187–88) **Using the ellipsis mark**

1. My father was dying . . . what would happen to us?
2. Our lives would have been different if . . . .

■ **Exercise 7** (p. 188) **Using end marks, commas, colons, dashes, and parentheses**

Answers may vary somewhat.

1. same: aluminum guardrails, green signs, white lettering.
2. "Is it—is it the green light then?" was all I managed to say.
3. again: What . . . theater.
4. typo: "The . . . refugees."
5. "Judy!" she exploded. "Judy, that's . . . say."
   She raised . . . daughter, but it wouldn't reach.
6. Emily (formerly Mrs. Goyette) caught . . . urgently.

7. wished to be—a professional dancer.
8. thinkers—conservatives or liberals—who . . . human.
9. put it. "Rose Bowl, Sugar Bowl, and Orange Bowl—all are gravy bowls."
10. "very" ("I am good and mad"), and . . . coffee, not the cup, is hot.

18 Spelling and Hyphenation

Because spelling problems vary from student to student, no one approach to teaching spelling will help all students uniformly, but the six suggestions that begin Section **18** are sound advice to all writers. Whenever possible, instruction in spelling should be individualized to meet the needs of the class or, ideally, of each student.

One method is to compile a list of the three or four most frequently misspelled words in a set of themes and to present the words with appropriate spelling rules in the process of returning the themes. Working from students' writing, you are then sure to teach the words that need attending to rather than dwelling on words that cause the class little problem. Further, over the semester you might want to compile a class list; the words that recur in more than two sets of themes could be assigned for special study.

A second approach is to have students keep a list of words which they have misspelled in their writing. Rather than ask students to recopy the misspelling (which reinforces the error), have them write down the correct spelling and the rule or device which will help them remember the spelling. Such a list might look like this:

An Individual Spelling List

laid—like *said*	[analogy]
forfeit—not an *ee* sound	[rule reference]
minor—minority	[change of stress]
category—cat-e-gory	[syllabication]
recommend—re + commend	[structural analysis]
studying—y + ing	[rule reference]
together—to get her	[mnemonic device]
accept—to accept gifts	[use in context]

Spelling can be tested in a number of ways. Here are some suggestions:

1. Assign groups of twenty words a week chosen from the list of frequently misspelled words plus those on the class list; then dictate ten of them for the students to write down. This approach has the advantage of being quick, easy, and familiar; and students have said that it causes them to be more careful with all spellings as they prepare an essay.
2. Give each student several words to spell orally.
3. To test easily confused words, dictate words in context and ask students to write either the word or the phrase.
4. Ask students to write a paragraph using selected words.
5. Write a multiple-choice quiz, asking students to select the one misspelled word from a series of three to five words, or the one correctly spelled word from a series of misspelled words.

In short, spelling is a skill that students who want their ideas to be taken seriously must master, but testing spelling need not be limited to a single method.

For section **18e** two cautions are in order. First, students should realize that not all words ending in *f* or *fe* change the ending to *ve* before adding *s* (*safes, proofs, beliefs, handkerchiefs*); some have two plural forms (*hoofs, hooves; scarfs, scarves*). Second, they should realize that *-es* (not *-s*) marks the plural in such words as *tomatoes* and *potatoes;* thus, *tomatoe* and *potatoe* are incorrect singular forms.

ACTIVITIES

1. Have students pronounce correctly each word listed in **18a.** Ask students what mispronunciation they hear in the speech of others (not, of course, in their speech or that of their classmates). Some frequent mispronunciations are:

athlete	drowned	pertain	recognize
barbarous	escape	prescribe	represent
candidate	everything	probable	quantity or quanity
disastrous	gratitude	relevant	umbrella

2. Have students choose the correct forms:

   a. If you expect to (*accept, except*) their dinner invitation, I'd (*advice, advise*) you to (*choose, chose*) some loosely fitting (*clothes, cloths*).

   b. They usually serve five or six (*coarses, courses*) (*altogether, all together*), and the table setting (*always, all ways*) (*complements, compliments*) the food. Not even the diet-(*conscience, conscious*) are unimpressed by the (*desert, dessert*)—raspberry torte.

   c. (*Sense, Since*) you can do no better (*than, then*) to dine in the (*presence, presents*) of such (*holy, wholly*) gracious hosts, my (*council, counsel*) is to (*precede, proceed*) with your plans to attend what (*maybe, may be*) a (*lessen, lesson*) in attention to every (*miner, minor*) detail.

   d. Use (*your, you're*) best (*stationary, stationery*) to (*rite, write, right*) a thank-you note; a genuine (*complement, compliment*) (*formerly, formally*) given is (*all ways, always*) welcome.

3. Ask students to use hyphenated words as adjectives in listing five qualities that describe their ideal spouse (such as *bluegrass-loving cowboy, well-groomed botanist, a wife with a one-day-at-a-time philosophy of life*). Also ask students to use five *-ly*-adverb-adjective combinations to describe their ideal instructor (*basically optimistic adult, totally organized lecturer*).

ANSWERS TO EXERCISES

■ **Exercise 1** (pp. 196–97)   **Adding suffixes**

1. likely, safely, surely
2. excitable, exciting, excitement
3. careful, hopeful, useful
4. arguing, argument, arguable
5. coming, noticing, hoping
6. using, useless
7. continuous, courageous
8. completely, completing
9. desirable, noticeable
10. managing, management

■ **Exercise 2** (p. 197)   **Forming present participles and past tense**

1. admitting, admitted
2. bragging, bragged
3. concealing, concealed
4. gripping, gripped
5. hoping, hoped
6. jogging, jogged
7. planning, planned
8. rebelling, rebelled
9. stopping, stopped
10. auditing, audited

■ **Exercise 3** (p. 198)   **Adding suffixes**

1. variable, pliable
2. funnier, carrier
3. various, luxurious
4. easily, finally
5. supplied, stayed
6. studying, worrying
7. paid, laid
8. livelihood, likelihood
9. friendliness, loneliness
10. usually, coolly

■ **Exercise 4** (p. 198)   **Spelling with *ei* and *ie***

1. piece
2. achieve
3. receive
4. neigh
5. freight
6. apiece
7. belief
8. conceive
9. their
10. deceit
11. niece
12. shield
13. weird
14. shriek
15. priest

■ **Exercise 5** (p. 200)   **Forming plurals**

1. beliefs
2. theories
3. churches
4. geniuses [RARE: genii for "spirits"]
5. Kellys
6. baths
7. heroes
8. stories
9. wishes
10. forties
11. radiuses OR radii
12. scarves OR scarfs
13. wives

14. speeches
15. tomatoes
16. phenomena OR phenomenons
17. halos OR haloes
18. children
19. handfuls
20. rodeos

■ **Exercise 6** (p. 208)   **Using the hyphen**

 1. a six-room apartment
 2. mind-exhausting examinations
 3. ink-stained fingers
 4. an eighteen-year-old voter
 5. budget-minded shoppers
 6. hundred-dollar tents
 7. all-night peace talks
 8. a teacher-training program
 9. a flag-waving hitchhiker
10. lily-covered ponds

■ **Exercise 7** (p. 209)   **Using needed hyphens**

 1. self-respect
 2. scorekeepers
 3. sugar-cured bacon
 4. a profit-sharing plan
 5. a nightlatch
 6. twenty-four
 7. an all-purpose cleaner
 8. a ninety-two-year-old woman
 9. V-shaped
10. snow-covered fences
11. the Montreal-Portland flight
    OR the Montreal-to-Portland flight
12. a two-or-three-day sale

19   Good Usage and Glossary

The activities suggested here and in the titles listed in the "Diction and Usage" section of the annotated bibliography should provide ample material for the use of the dictionary and for usage appropriate to formal writing.

You could use either or both of the following misconceptions to begin a discussion of lexicography and attitudes toward language:

1. *A modern dictionary tells us how words should be used.* Ask students what they understand *should be used* to mean. Students who have been told to "look it up in the dictionary" accept information in it without much question and without knowing anything about the philosophy which has guided the making of it. Students see a dictionary as the authority on words, but few know whether their dictionaries are prescriptive or descriptive; in fact, few know the difference between prescriptive and descriptive views of language or are aware of any differences between dictionaries. A brief survey of lexicographers' attitudes toward language will introduce students to the decisions that go into the writing of entries.

2. *Grammar is the way words should be used.* Grammar is the study of the system or structure of English; usage is the study of the ways words are actually used. Thus, case and agreement are matters of grammar (How does English show possessive case? How does English show pronoun-antecedent agreement?). Usage is the study of the conventional, rather than the systematic, side of language (What words characterize the region the speaker lives in? What is the difference between *compare to* and *compare with?* Are *fewer* and *less* interchangeable in formal writing?).

To illustrate the difference, *ain't* (a contraction of *am not*) is grammatically correct in the first-person singular, but is labeled "nonstandard" because speakers of standard English find it unacceptable. *Ain't I* is a negative interrogative, analogous to *aren't we,* but it is nevertheless not a part of standard English. On the other hand, *aren't I,* one alternative to *ain't I,* is ungrammatical (*are not I*) but it is a usage accepted by speakers of standard English.

As an introduction to a few basic principles of language study, such assumptions as the following give beginning writers perspective on language:

1. Language is symbolic.
2. Living languages change.
3. Language has system.
4. Language has hierarchies (sound, syllable, word, sentence, paragraph).

    5. Speech, not writing, is primary; writing is the graphic representation of sounds.

For a discussion of common but incorrect notions about language, see "Facts, Assumptions, and Misconceptions About Language," Chapter 1 of Thomas Pyles' and John Algeo's *The Origins and Development of the English Language* (3rd edition, 1982).

Once students realize that languages change, they are ready for dictionary study to see how those changes are recorded. The goal is for students to learn about the problems lexicographers must solve, the parts of a dictionary, the advantages and disadvantages of several desk dictionaries, and the variety of English dictionaries (slang, Americanisms, usage, etc.) and specialized dictionaries. Most important, however, students should come to see words as "integers" (Thoreau).

As part of this unit on dictionaries, the usage terms merit particular attention. Students should be aware that lexicographers do not always agree about which usage label, if any, to give a word; and students should make sure that they understand the differences between such terms as *colloquial, regional,* and *informal.* The *American Heritage Dictionary,* for instance, includes these labels (pp. xlvi–xlvii):

    1. *nonstandard*—for words not considered part of "standard, educated speech"
    2. *informal*—for words "acceptable in conversation . . . [but] not . . . suitable in formal writing"
    3. *slang*—for informal, usually short-lived, words whose aim is "to produce rhetorical effect, such as incongruity, irreverence, or exaggeration"
    4. *vulgar*—for taboo words
    5. *obsolete*—for words "no longer used except in quotation or intentional archaism"
    6. *archaic*—for words "that once were common, but are currently rare and are readily identifiable as belonging to a style of language no longer in general use"
    7. *rare*—for words used infrequently because their synonyms are used instead
    8. *poetic*—for words common to poetry but not to prose
    9. *regional*—for words used by or associated with one particular area

Other labels commonly used by lexicographers are *colloquial, dialect, illiterate, substandard,* and *technical.* Students should consult their dictionaries for a list of usage or status labels.

Finally, the study of usage and attitudes toward language provides a logical and convenient opportunity to discuss sexism in language.

One way to begin is to ask how sexism affects the decisions writers make and then to examine ways to avoid demeaning either the subject of the essay or the audience by inappropriate word choices or images. (McGraw-Hill's well-known pamphlet "Guidelines For Equal Treatment of the Sexes" provides principles and many specific examples to help writers solve problems of sex discrimination in writing.)

ACTIVITIES

1. These two lists are supplements to Exercise 5. Have students give the etymology of each of the following words:

   a. aloof   a. cartel
   b. cereal   b. dollar
   c. gargle   c. glamour
   d. grape   d. gossip
   e. laser   e. lieutenant
   f. sideburns   f. meander
   g. telethon   g. suede
   h. turnpike   h. vinegar
   i. tuxedo   i. wacky
   j. tycoon   j. zoo

2. Have students use their dictionaries to identify the languages from which each of the following words was borrowed:

   a. bungalow   f. mosquito
   b. chocolate   g. succotash
   c. flamboyant   h. taboo
   d. gruff   i. yam
   e. judo   j. yogurt

3. Ask students to mark the root and the prefix or suffix of each word; then have students use the root and another affix to form a word:

   a. underground   f. creative
   b. admit   g. judgment
   c. converse   h. circumvent
   d. bisect   i. vision
   e. interlock   j. propel

4. Give students an opportunity to compare dictionaries while they learn about the kinds of information dictionaries contain. Have

students bring a standard college dictionary to class. Begin the class by asking for the name of each dictionary and listing the titles on the chalkboard. Then ask students to help list the kinds of information contained in an entry: spelling, syllabication, pronunciation, stress, variant spellings, variant pronunciations, abbreviations, inflected forms, etymology, definitions (ordered by most common meaning or by historical order), part(s) of speech, usage label, examples of the word in context, synonyms, antonyms, usage notes. Shift attention from the entry to the entire dictionary by asking if the dictionaries contain the following and if so, where:

> abbreviations
> foreign terms
> geographical names
> population figures
> male and female first names
> names of famous people
> names and locations of U.S. colleges and universities
> charts of weights and measures
> illustrations
> forms of address in letters to public figures
> a history of English
> a chart of Indo-European and non-Indo-European languages
> a glossary or usage labels
> a chart of pronunciation symbols [Call attention to differences in the use of symbols by asking students for the symbols of the sounds italicized here: *thing, sharp, justify, father, ask,* and *urge.*]

5. Have students consult their dictionaries for:

   a. the preferred pronunciations of *aunt, creek, exquisite, harass*
   b. the plurals of *criterion, elk, parenthesis, voodoo*
   c. the number of meanings for *in, plastic,* and *run* (verb)
   d. the usage label, if any, for *ain't, bib and tucker, keckle, once-over, potlatch, you-all, yummy*
   e. the parts of speech for *best, but, while*

6. Using the dialect survey in Roger W. Shuy's *Discovering American Dialects,* have students identify their speech and discuss why it is more difficult to define their dialects than those of their grandparents' time. Ask whether they think regional varieties of English will disappear.

7. Have students compile a dictionary of slang used by the students at their college or university. Ask them to label terms used only at that school.

8. Have students collect examples of jargon or gobbledygook and, for one example, provide a translation in plain English. The two examples here illustrate the kind of language students should look for:

   a. Rarely have I known, hither-to, the unalloyed pleasure of being the recipient of so concentrated a demonstration of domestic felicity as was lavished upon this unsuspecting beneficiary of your matchless hospitality. Truly, your hearth is a lodestone for the weary wayfarer, and your threshold an entrance to unimaginable delights.

      —a Hallmark thank-you card

   b. Walking through the Soils Building at the University of Wisconsin in Madison, I stopped in front of a display case containing unusual soil and mineral specimens. One descriptive card read:

      "Structure built by an avian engineer using solid waste (plastic, paper, tin foil); organic debris from vegetation; and mineral soil. The soil was compacted into a platy, stratified deposit which is essentially a series of crusts of reduced hydraulic conductivity. The structure, a segment of a concretion, is formed on a tree branch close to the canopy. It is an epiphytic pedological feature, whose fate is to be translocated by free fall to the soil surface, where it will eventually be incorporated into the soil, except that part which decomposes first."

      Displayed in the glass case was a robin's nest.

      —*Reader's Digest*

9. Have students write down a simple, brief sentence or familiar saying. Then ask them to translate it into jargon or gobbledygook. Ask students to read their jargon-sentence for others to decipher.

10. Ask students to compile examples of jargon used by one group (such as CB owners, grocery clerks, fast-food employees, computer programmers, pilots, or sailors) and to write a paragraph using as much of that jargon as possible.

11. Have students revise the following sentences according to the principles of formal usage:

a. All the farther I had yet to drive seems to be alot since I had already driven four hundred miles that day.

b. Its an awful long ways from South Dakota to Pennsylvania, especially on these kind of roads, when you're kinda tired plus you're suppose to be there before dinner time because your folks are waiting on you.

c. Be sure and stop in Milwaukee if you're fixing to have a fun vacation.

d. Hopefully, it's okay to show up unannounced if the visit's just only for a couple of hours.

e. No amount of coaxing will make me liable to accept an itinerary that's different than the one Lee and myself planned. The reason is because the perfect vacation is an allusion alright, but each and every summer the affects of all them glossy summer-vacation brochures gets us to making plans for a trip superior than last year's.

ANSWERS TO EXERCISES

Note: No answers are given for the dictionary exercises in this section, as answers will vary according to the dictionary used.

■ **Exercise 9** (pp. 223–24)   **Rewriting to eliminate jargon**

Answers will vary. The following are possibilities.

1. The lot is too steep for a playground.
2. Mr. Blank has replied that he will not accept the promotion.
3. The Public Health Service will pay for dental work needed by medical patients in the hospital.
4. I give you this orange.
5. I like short, clear words.
6. We are coming to realize that teachers, parents, and students must work together to improve the curriculum.

20 Exactness

Consider the writer's task: to transfer via words the ideas and images in his or her mind to an audience with no immediate opportunity to ask questions about what the writer has said. And if that were not enough, consider some other possible obstacles:

1. uncertainty about what to say or how to say it

2. unconventional use of words, either because of errors in grammar or usage or because of an overly personalized language

3. a complex message

4. an audience hostile to prose and/or to the subject

5. audience distractions (television, the smell of food, conversation, a fire siren)

6. the differences between writer and audience in values, background, education, and experience

7. an audience using definitions of key words different from the writer's

Conscientious writers assume two things: first, that the message and the audience must both be considered and second, that if readers can misread or misunderstand, they will (sometimes going so far as to lose the meaning entirely). The choice of exact words is one important method for increasing the likelihood of the message's being interpreted as the writer conceived it.

The use of figurative language is another method by which writers make meaning exact. Metaphors and similes clarify the nature of something unknown or unfamiliar by comparing it to something familiar. For instance, the simile "an effusive apology as cloying as the perfume of a roomful of lilacs during a June piano recital" explains that the lengths of the apology (the unfamiliar) are like a heavy perfume in a warm, crowded room (the familiar). In both cases the excesses go beyond what is desirable—too much apology is like too much perfume. Metaphors also attempt an exact comparison, but the reader must identify the two items (no *like* or *as* to guide the way) as well as the point of comparison. For example, in "his tightly knit prose" the metaphor compares the intricacies of two structures: the securely intertwined loops of a sweater (the familiar) and the coherence of the author's writing (unfamiliar); the structure of both results from the pattern of connections.

Clichés are figurative language gone stale. Comparisons once fresh but now routine complete the cycle of originate-use-discard that metaphors and similes go through. The comparison arises because a writer needs a vigorous, striking, new image that exactly describes the bond between familiar and unfamiliar. If the comparison is effective, others adopt it until so many people are using it that it no longer is considered strikingly exact. Thus it becomes a cliché, and writers must create new expressions.

A third way to achieve exactness of meaning is to use allusions. The purpose of linking familiar phrases from literature or the Bible with the writer's idea is to make a point or connect ideas in a way no other words or references could. Such citations are valuable only if the audience recognizes them and understands how they make the writer's meaning exact. For example, the sentence ''Apparently believing that his sound and fury signified something, the incensed customer continued his harangue'' contains a reference to Macbeth's words, but the reader must recognize the allusion and the difference between the original speech and the words in this sentence in order to understand the irony of the man's continuing harangue. Of course, allusions used to pad ideas or to show off the writer's background should not be included.

ACTIVITIES

1. To make vivid the point that a variety of interpretations of a given word are possible, ask students to close their eyes (but to stay awake) and to listen to the next word or phrase spoken. After the instructor says the word *dog,* it's time to have students describe what they pictured when the word was said. The instructor should ask questions to help students describe the image precisely (breed, size, color, age, name, stance). Repeat the exercise using *tree* and then *gates of heaven* to illustrate the range of experiences and backgrounds that color the images of what are perceived as simple words.

2. On the chalkboard write this sentence: *Lynn walked into the room.* Give students a few seconds to think of several synonyms for *walk* and then call on every student (row by row) for a word to add to the list. Collecting forty or more words provides ample opportunity to discuss connotation. The exercise may be repeated by collecting synonyms for *said* or by asking males to list synonyms for *female* and females to list synonyms for *male.* The latter exercise leads naturally into a discussion of what the various connotations suggest about how the sexes view each other.

3. Have students identify the similes, metaphors, or personification in the following sentences and comment on the effectiveness of each:

   a. "Nina Brett's laugh was like tiny ice cubes falling into a thin glass from a great height."—Gail Godwin, *Glass People*

   b. "Like any encyclopedia, a great cathedral cannot be read at a glance. If one's time is limited, it is best to concentrate on a few particularly glorious chapters. At Bourges, these are the center portal of the west facade and the windows. These should be read slowly, with the aid of good binoculars."—*New York Times*, April 19, 1981

   c. "A man and a woman . . . were staring up at a large black-and-white photograph of the great galaxy of Andromeda, a pinwheel of billions of stars that . . . was similar to our galaxy. . . ."—*New York Times*, April 19, 1981

   d. "Such words and phrases [politicians' coinages] are but the insects of a season at the most."—George Campbell, *The Philosophy of Rhetoric*

   e. " . . . the remarkable boundary between the lush green of the land blessed by the Nile's water and the barren, brown desert beyond the reach of irrigation. So clear and absolute is this line that from the air it looks as if a child has put down his crayons after doing just part of a coloring book's page."—*New York Times*, May 24, 1981

   f. "Adjective salad is delicious, with each element contributing its individual and unique flavor; but a puree of adjective soup tastes yecchy."—William Safire, *On Language*

4. Have students make a list of metaphors that use names of parts of the body. Such metaphors include:

the *eye* of a hurricane	an *ear* of corn
the *brow* of a hill	the *foot* of a bed
the *nose* of an airplane	the *tongue* of a shoe
the *heart* of the matter	the *ribs* of a ship
bald cypress *knees*	the *hands* of a clock
the *face* of a cliff	the *elbow* of a river
a fine-*toothed* comb	a *cheeky* reply

   Ask students to create similes for five of the italicized words. Or ask students to make a list of foods used metaphorically. Examples might include:

cauliflower ears	a bread-and-butter note	
in a pickle	peach	
in a jam	peanut	
in a stew	shrimp	
a beefy wrangler	string bean	metaphors for people
a corny joke	honey	
salt-and-pepper hair	tomato	

5. Have students select words to complete the chart.

General	Specific	More Specific/Concrete
sport	_____	_____
_____	noun	_____
relationship	_____	_____
_____	_____	French fries
_____	perennials	_____

6. Have students compile a list of euphemisms associated with death and funerals and then write a paragraph using as many of them as possible.

ANSWERS TO EXERCISES

Note: No answers are given for the dictionary exercises in this section, as answers will vary according to the dictionary used.

■ **Exercise 1** (pp. 247–48)   **Correcting errors in diction and using exact words**

1. compost
2. so OR ; therefore
3. injustice
4. adapted
5. very friendly / courteous / polite   [Answers will vary.]
6. unfortunate
7. but OR ; however
8. intimated
9. seasonal
10. affects

21   Wordiness

Direct prose concentrates on the straightforward statement of ideas; nothing intervenes between ideas and precise diction. Economical prose wastes no words, thus keeping ideas vigorous; every word is spent profitably. The most ideas for the fewest words is the writer's goal; for just as one cup of tomato paste contains a tomato flavor more distilled than that in one cup of tomato juice, so direct, economical prose contains ideas more distilled than those in wordy prose.

In addition to diluting thoughts, wordy prose has other disadvantages. It shows the writer's inability to control the expression of ideas. It shows lack of respect for exact diction and for the audience, since wordy prose requires more time to read than economical prose. Compare, for example, the reading times of *After due consideration, the answer is affirmative* and *Yes*. In short, flabby diction is evidence of poor sentence tone.

Once beginning writers identify wordiness in their own prose, they are ready for systematic revisions. Simply cutting words often produces awkward or choppy sentences and restricts revision to one technique for intra-sentence problems. However, a method that applies omitting, rearranging, and combining within and between sentences gives writers an orderly series of options. The following steps outline one approach:

1. A compound predicate is reduced to one predicate.

    a. They *called* her *up* and *asked* her to advise them about selecting roses for a hedge.
    b. They *asked* her advice about selecting roses for a hedge.

2. A main clause becomes a subordinate clause.

    a. They asked her advice about selecting roses for a hedge.
    b. *When they asked her advice about selecting roses for a hedge,* she recommended floribundas for a hedge that would bloom continuously.

3. A subordinate clause becomes a phrase.

    a. When they asked her *what roses to select for a hedge,* she recommended floribundas for a hedge *that would bloom continuously.*
    b. When they asked her about *selecting roses for a hedge,* she recommended floribundas for a hedge *of continuous blooms.*

4. A phrase becomes a word.

   a. When they asked her about *selecting roses for a hedge,* she recommended floribundas *for a hedge of continuous blooms.*
   b. When they asked her about *hedge roses,* she recommended *continuously blooming floribundas.*

5. Several words become one or are omitted entirely.

   a. When they asked *her* about *suggested* hedge roses, she *really strongly* recommended *a hedge of continuously everblooming* floribundas.
   b. When they asked about hedge roses, she recommended floribundas.

6. One sentence combines with another.

   a. When they asked about hedge roses, she recommended floribundas. She thought that for red roses they might like such varieties as "Europeana," "Vogue," and "Eutin."
   b. When they asked about hedge roses, she recommended three red floribundas: "Europeana," "Vogue," and "Eutin."
   c. "Europeana," "Vogue," and "Eutin" were the three varieties of red floribunda she recommended for their hedge.
   d. She recommended three red floribundas—"Europeana," "Vogue," and "Eutin"—for their hedge.

ACTIVITIES

1. Have students use direct, economical prose to revise these sentences:

   a. There are quite a few preparations at home to get ready for even today's modern picnic.
   b. The last and final step is the job of loading the necessities and things into the car. In this day and age the necessities often include Frisbees and volleyballs along with the food. This is done so that people will have something to do before the meal.
   c. After the windy gust, all the Styrofoam cups and paper plates on the picnic table were in an upset position. The major reason why they were was because Beth hadn't had time to fill the cups with lemonade drinks and lay the silverware on the plates.

2. No amount of exercises replaces having students reduce the word-iness in their own prose. To reduce the routine of the one-writer–one-essay class hour, use a variety of approaches and have students work with sentences and paragraphs (reserve the revision of entire essays for homework assignments).

    a. Have students number and write out or type (double space to allow room for revisions) sentences from one paragraph of a recent theme. Then ask students to revise each sentence two ways. Have students exchange papers and check the rewritten sentences for wordiness. Finally, have the writer use the revised and corrected sentences in a paragraph.
    b. Bring to class a handout of wordy sentences from students' writing. Ask students to eliminate the wordiness and tell which of the six steps they used.
    c. Have pairs of students revise a paragraph of each other's to eliminate wordiness.
    d. Have two students work separately to revise the same paragraph; then as a class, discuss which revisions are more effective. If pairing students would result in more than six or seven sets of paragraphs to discuss, consider having groups of three to six students work together to produce one revised paragraph.

ANSWERS TO EXERCISES

■ Exercise 1 (p. 264)   Revising to eliminate wordiness

Answers will vary somewhat.

1. As a rule, government officials express concern about public interest, but it takes a crisis to get them to act.
2. Good health is essential.
3. During the last two innings, many senseless mistakes occurred.
4. When combined, these ingredients make a nutritious one-dish meal.
5. The exact date is not known.
6. Long lines of starving refugees were helped by Red Cross volunteers.
7. Judy delights in giving parties.
8. Perhaps the chief cause of obesity is lack of exercise.
9. Only beginners can enter that contest.
10. The skyscrapers form a silhouette against the evening sky.

■ **Exercise 2** (p. 264) **Substituting one or two words for long phrases**

1. before
2. now OR today OR nowadays
3. appeared
4. can work
5. died
6. soon OR before long
7. similar to OR like
8. expensive
9. seriously OR somewhat seriously
10. about $2500

■**Exercise 3** (p. 265) **Striking out unnecessary words**

Answers may vary somewhat.

1. It seems obvious.
2. I stayed behind because I had no money.
3. Last Saturday afternoon I bought a sailboat, a nice yellow toy.
4. All these oil slicks, massive or not, do damage to the environment.
5. As for biased newscasts, I realize that reporters have to do some editing, though they may not use the finest judgment when underscoring some stories and downplaying others.

■ **Exercise 4** (p. 266–67) **Condensing sentences**

1. These are dangerous pitfalls.
2. This is an aggressive act.
3. It was a carefully planned garden.
4. It was a passionately delivered speech.
5. Her husband's dishes are not as good as her father's.
6. The students' ideas were different from the advertiser's.
7. Inevitably, corporations produce goods to make a profit.
8. Predictably, before an election legislators reduce taxation to win the approval of voters.
9. A pro-labor group wants two-month vacations.
10. One anti-"nuke" editorial stressed the need for state-controlled plants.

■ **Exercise 5** (p. 267) **Reducing the number of words**

Answers will vary. The following are possibilities.

1. These invisible hazards cause many fatal accidents.
2. The United States was being invaded by foreign investors buying up farms.
3. Although my parents did not approve, I married Evelyn last June.
4. The fire chief recommended that wooden shingles not be used on homes.
5. Many on the jury considered Smith's lawyer incompetent.

■ **Exercise 6** (pp. 269–70) **Eliminating needless repetition and clumsy synonyms**

Answers will vary. The following are possibilities.

1. The President's recommendation to Congress sounded outlandish.
2. The condition of the floors after I had painted the ceiling shocked my wife.
3. Unexpected interruptions like that derail my thoughts.
4. A comedy of intrigue (or of situation) relies on action rather than on characterization.
5. We had to stay at Gate 13 for hours.
6. Brunch is a blend of *breakfast* and *lunch; fantabulous,* of *fantastic* and *fabulous.*
7. A new storage room was added to the side of the house.
8. A debater in action should make the best use of time.
9. Leslie likes to go to the mountains to ski, Marcia to fish, and Joseph to meditate. OR Leslie likes to go to the mountains to ski; Marcia, to fish; and Joseph, to meditate.
10. Numerous products can be made from tobacco. Its nicotine is used in pesticides, and its sugar helps control blood pressure.

■ **Exercise 7** (p. 270) **Eliminating wordiness and useless repetition**

1. The manager returned the application because of illegible handwriting.
2. It is difficult today to find a chemist who shows as much promise as Joseph Blake.
3. From time to time, a person needs to remember that anybody who is learning to walk has to put one foot before the other.
4. A distant hurricane or a seaquake can cause a tidal wave.
5. The National Gallery of Art in Washington, D.C., which houses the Mellon, Kress, and Widener collections, is one of the world's largest marble structures.
6. In my family, schoolwork came first, chores second, fun and games next, and discussions last.
7. Neither the auto nor the steel industry relished the thought of Americans importing tens of thousands of cars.
8. The backlash that followed the Supreme Court ruling was stronger than I had expected.
9. The yelling of fans in the stadium is so deafening that I stay home and watch the games on TV.

10. One reason these two newspapers are so powerful is that people are happy to let reporters and editors tell them what to think.

22   Omission of Necessary Words

Whether omissions of necessary words result from the hurried, inaccurate recording of thoughts or the accurate recording of speech patterns, the effect on the audience is the same—a sentence that reads awkwardly and withholds a complete idea, thereby distracting the reader's attention until the omitted word is restored.

Three errors should receive special attention since they are made by students who usually proofread carefully for other omissions:

1. Prepositions omitted after verbs or other words (*neither amused* [*by*] *nor interested in any explanation; overcome* [*by*] *and grateful for the comforting words; along* [*with*] *or in place of the salad*).

2. Elements in a comparison omitted. Comparisons are complete when the two subjects and the point of comparison are present. Thus, in the example in **22c,** *snow here* and *snow in Miami* are the subjects and *scarcity* is the point of comparison. But a sentence like *Wool is better for carpets* lacks the second subject, so that the point of comparison (*better*) is meaningless, yet such sentences occur frequently in commercial advertising as well as in students' writing.

3. Comma misused after *such.* When *such* is used as an intensifier, it is not separated from its clause by a comma (*He owns such a successful herbal tea company that he was a millionaire before he was thirty*). A comma is needed, however, when *such* occurs in parenthetical lists of examples (*Campers enjoy the outdoors in many ways, such as hiking, fishing, and birdwatching*).

ACTIVITIES

1. See Pence and Emery, *A Grammar of Present-Day English,* 2nd ed. (Macmillan, 1963), for a list of prepositions used idiomati-

cally. Ask students to use selected prepositions in sentences that illustrate differences in meaning (such as *adapted to, adapted from; need for, need of; compare to, compare with*).

2. Have students collect and rewrite examples of incomplete comparisons used in ads.

3. Ask students to write—but not to punctuate—sentences illustrating *such* used as an intensifier and as the head of a parenthetical list. Have students write the sentences on the board and ask others to provide the punctuation.

ANSWERS TO EXERCISES

■ **Exercise 1** (p. 273)   **Supplying needed words**

1. brewing *in* the
2. Sheila *that* Richard
3. kind *of* course
4. *During the* winter
5. was *that* my / pair *of* shoes
6. ask *for* nor
7. Fires *that* [OR *which*] had
8. dollar *and* [OR *but*] then
9. referred *to* was OR book *to* which
10. variety *of* spices
11. saw *that* the OR boy *who* finally
12. exception *that* [OR *which*] proves

■ **Exercise 2** (p. 273)   **Supplying needed words**

1. The; the; a
2. that OR which
3. that
4. of; who; of; who

■ **Exercise 3** (p. 275)   **Supplying needed words**

1. They *have* [OR *had*] been trying
2. The consumers *had* better listen
3. Ed's income is less than *that of* his wife.
   OR Ed's income is less than his wife*'s*.
4. Bruce admires Cathy more than Aline *does*.
   OR Bruce admires Cathy more than *he does* Aline.

5. Fiberglass roofs are better *than these.* [Answers will vary.]
6. as any *other* place.
7. I always have *liked*
8. One argument was as bad *as*
9. The ordinance never has *been*
10. more than the cranky young nurse *does.*
    OR more than *he does* the cranky young nurse.

■ **Exercise 4** (p. 276)   **Supplying needed words**

Answers may vary somewhat. The following are possibilities.

1. I had *in* my senior year a strange type *of* virus.
2. As far as Boston *is concerned,* I could see *that* the people
3. The group is opposed *to*
4. I wish I *had* been able to play football at *the* university.
5. a person *who* has a similar problem.
6. His assistant and *his* close friend
7. The trouble is *that*
8. He entered *the* American Institute for Foreign Trade *in* 1949.
9. more than *he paid* Jim.
    OR more than Jim *did.*
10. Nick announced *that*
11. as mild as *that in* Louisiana.
    OR as mild as Louisiana*'s.*
12. mysteries like *those involving* Sherlock Holmes
13. the hole *through* which the rabbit escaped.
14. If Jack goes into a profession *for* which
15. The lawyer had to prove *that*
16. I *have* been
17. These trainees know *that* they *had* better study.
18. people, and *they were* still coming.
19. Nobody *is* interested *in* their problems.
20. Elizabeth saw *that* Nell was not in *the* room.

23   Unity and Logical Thinking

Sometimes students assume that because an essay is neatly typed and grammatically and mechanically correct it is also logically organized and soundly reasoned. That non sequitur then traps them into believing that a neat manuscript will conceal any faults in the writer's thinking.

Sentences that lack unity betray the writer's commitment to the central idea. While unrelated detail is probably more easily identified than excessive detail, students should understand that both undermine the effectiveness of the sentence—one by introducing extraneous material and the other by overwhelming the central idea in an attempt to provide adequate development for it. Apparently unrelated ideas are difficult for writers to identify since they understand the relationship and believe that what is obvious to them is obvious to the audience. A simple two-part question will help students avoid the problems: What is the relationship among ideas and how have I indicated it?

An awkward definition (*Success is if you achieve your goal*) can be corrected by reviewing the parts of a formal definition (classification and differentiation or general category and distinguishing characteristics) and phrasing the definition so that the word being defined and the word identifying the classification are grammatically parallel (*Success is the achievement of a desired goal*).

A mixed construction, which results from the use of parts of at least two possible statements, can be corrected by having students sort out the possibilities and choose the one they judge more effective. Here are two examples (From Exercise 3):

> Because his feet are not the same size explains the difficulty he has finding shoes that fit.
> 1. Because his feet are not the same size, he has difficulty finding shoes that fit.
> 2. Having feet that are not the same size explains the difficulty he has finding shoes that fit.

> Does anyone here know why George resigned or where did he find a better job?
> 1. Does anyone here know why George resigned or where he found a better job?
> 2. Why did George resign and where did he find a better job?

After seeing the alternatives, students may decide that neither choice is as effective as they would like and produce other sentences.

Teaching the elements of sound reasoning without directly attacking students' own illogical arguments (and thus provoking them to illogical defenses) need not mean using dull examples or ignoring students' reasoning processes. In fact, drawing upon decisions students are commonly faced with helps them to master the principles in Section 23 before they examine the logic of their writing. Using registration, for example, the instructor might ask students to draw up a list of the pros and cons for enrolling in this particular section of Freshman Composition during the current semester:

Pro

1. I'd have to get up earlier for the other sections.
2. It's the only hour that doesn't interfere with my work schedule.
3. My roommate's also taking it at this hour.
4. The computer put me here.
5. It was in the same building as my next class.

Con

1. There's too much writing, and I don't like writing.
2. English teachers are always criticizing us conservatives.
3. I need a good grade-point average this semester.
4. Friends say that this instructor grades too hard.

During the discussion of the logic of the reasons, the students don't need to admit to having used any of them to make their own decision, but the experiences of the class (and of their friends) will be represented. After the discussion, students might volunteer the reasons they chose the section and, if they wish, discuss the logic involved.

After the students have examined their own decision-making, they are better able to examine the decisions of others to support or oppose popular issues; here it is important not that students agree with the decisions but that they analyze the logic of the argument. Finally, students should examine their position on one popular issue (sufficiently narrowed and clearly defined) by discussing the logic of the reasons they have listed. Once they are sure that the reasons are logically sound, they may proceed to argue them in an essay.

ACTIVITIES

1. Ask students to list and discuss the pros and cons of: renting an apartment rather than a dorm room; attending summer school rather than working full time during the summer; attending their present school rather than a close rival; going to college immediately after high school graduation rather than waiting a year or so. Ask them to identify any logical fallacies in the reasons.

2. Have students use logical fallacies to write commercials for products of their choice.

3. Have students contrast the assumptions of arguments given by opposing sides on some campus issue.

4. After students have listed fifteen to twenty details about themselves, have them include every detail that will show them in a positive way in a single sentence. Ask them to write another sentence that shows them in a positive way but to select only those details that will make the point most emphatically. Have them discuss the effects of the two sentences. Then ask students to write a sentence using details that will create a negative impression, and finally, one that lacks unity, so that the reader can form no clear impression.

5. Ask students to write formal definitions for three slang words—one noun, one verb, and one adjective.

ANSWERS TO EXERCISES

■ **Exercise 1** (pp. 279–80)   **Rewriting to relate ideas**

Answers will vary. The following are possibilities.

1. Although I know that the visiting professor has different and refreshing views, I decided to miss the lecture on September 20 and to play badminton.
2. I hate strong windstorms that cause pecans to pelt my bedroom roof all night.
3. The fence and barn need repairs, but property taxes are so high that I cannot afford to improve the place.
4. There are so many types of bores at social gatherings that I prefer quiet evenings at home.
5. A telephone lineman who works during heavy storms can prove a hero. Of course, cowards can be found in any walk of life.
6. Jones was advised to hire a tutor in French immediately. Long hours of work at a service station kept his grades low.
7. Professor Stetson, who likes to draw parallels between modern men and literary characters, pointed out that Macbeth was not the only man to succumb to ambition.
8. Brad sent his sister a dozen red roses when she sang on a fifteen-minute program over KTUV.
9. Although the food in the cafeteria has been the subject of many jokes, most of the students who eat there do not look underfed.
10. During the summer, birds eat worms and insects that are pests to the farmer. In the fall, however, they migrate to the warmer countries.

■ **Exercise 2** (p. 281)   **Eliminating excessive detail**

Answers may vary somewhat. The following are possibilities.

1. During English class, we freshmen enjoyed discussing the implications of language in various advertisements.
2. The fan that Joan bought for her brother arrived today. He frets about any temperature that exceeds seventy.
3. When I was only four, I often walked alone the two miles between my house and the lake.
4. Four cars piled up on the freeway.
5. The senator advocated drastic reforms.
6. The boat, seaworthy ten years ago but dilapidated now, moved out into the bay.
7. Flames from the gas heater licked at the chintz curtains.
8. After finishing breakfast, Sigrid called the tree surgeon.
9. At last I returned the library book that I had used for my Tuesday report.
10. A course in business methods helps undergraduates to get jobs and tests their fitness for business.

■ **Exercise 3** (p. 283)   **Eliminating mixed or awkward constructions**

Answers will vary. The following are possibilities.

1. For Don, money does grow on trees, and he frequently shakes the limbs.
2. He has difficulty finding shoes that fit because his feet are not the same size.
3. Friction is the rubbing of one surface against another.
4. Several of the applicants brought their resumés with them.
5. One example of a ripoff would be the addition of a butcher's heavy thumb to the weight of the steak.
6. Like a bat guided by radar, Alexander avoided dangerous situations.
7. To be discreet is to carefully avoid saying or doing something tactless.
8. Does anyone here know why George resigned or where he found a better job?
9. Tourists are not permitted to bring their cameras indoors.
10. The need for glasses can cause a child to make mistakes in reading and writing.

24   Subordination

Students who have difficulty defining goals and managing their time to achieve them are also likely to have difficulty with subordinating ideas, for both activities require the ability to recognize and weigh priorities. Having a sense of the relative importance of ideas is prerequisite to using subordination.

Grammatically subordinate ideas are by no means necessarily of lesser rhetorical importance. Compare:

1. Sarah, who lived in Des Moines for six years, has just received her commercial pilot's license. [The subordinate element contains information unrelated to and of lesser importance than the main clause.]
2. As soon as Sarah flew to Seattle, Beth and I drove to Portland. [The subordinate clause establishes the time relationship and is just as important as the main clause.]
3. Although your request for a five-thousand-dollar raise has been denied, you will receive two more paid holidays. [The negative information in the subordinate clause is rhetorically more important than the positive information in the main clause.]

Grammatically coordinate ideas emphasize equal importance, although students often see coordination as a convenient way to link ideas without developing them. Believing that *and* is a transition that guarantees paragraph unity, beginning writers often link everything with *and*, creating prose that offers no relief for the reader no occasional bluffs or clumps of trees to punctuate the prairie.

ACTIVITIES

1. Ask students to write a main clause containing a subject, a verb, and a direct object. Have students exchange papers and add one subordinate clause. Repeat, again asking for a subordinate clause. Repeat, asking for one set of coordinate elements. Have students read and discuss the resulting sentences.

2. Ask students to write down three goals they want to achieve before the end of the semester. Have them rank the goals from most important to least important and then write a sentence using sub-

ordination to reflect the ranking. Ask them to follow the same procedure for three goals to be met within a year, three before they graduate, and three within five years after graduation.

3. Ask students to combine the following sentences in as many ways as possible and to identify which idea is stressed in each. Have them begin with coordination and then move to subordination.

   a. 1. I was walking through the park.
      2. An elderly lady was walking through the park.
      3. A thief stole the elderly lady's purse.

   b. 1. Marlene is a dentist.
      2. Her hobby is breeding tropical fish.
      3. Her husband is a film editor.
      4. His hobby is baking bread.

   c. 1. Eloise and Donald were waiting for a table.
      2. Two women dressed in evening gowns were seated at a table beside the window.
      3. A waiter spilled tangerine sherbet on one woman.

4. Too many elements in a sentence impede the main idea. Have students suggest revisions for these sentences:

   a. The family who bought that custom-designed ranch house that Avery Realty had on the market for eight months when sales were especially slow decided to ask that the previous owners return the water softener which was to remain in the house.

   b. Wearing the furry hat that his grandchildren who lived in Bismarck had given him when they learned that the only one he had was a green felt one that belonged to his brother who knew how cold North Dakota winters were, Carl walked to the diner where the owner cooked breakfast and said that a hungry man could eat three eggs as easily as two, so three eggs were what a customer would always get.

5. Have students use the suggestions for tightening sentences in Ken Macrorie's *Telling Writing* (Hayden Book Company, 1970) pages 25–31, to revise one or two paragraphs from a recent theme or from a draft of an upcoming theme.

ANSWERS TO EXERCISES

The following revisions are suggestions. Many other revisions for subordination are possible.

■ **Exercise 1** (p. 296)   **Using subordination to combine short sentences**

[1,2]Now that I have just read "The Idea of a University," I am especially interested in Newman's views regarding knowledge. [3,4,5]Newman says that knowledge is a treasure in itself, that it is its own reward, not just a means to an end. [6,7,8]Before reading this essay, I had looked upon knowledge only in terms of practical results—such as financial security. [9,10]Now I accept Newman's definition of knowledge, which is worth pursuing for its own sake.

■ **Exercise 2** (p. 297)   **Using Subordination to improve sentence unity**

1. After she had selected a lancet and sterilized it, she gave the patient a local anesthetic and lanced the infected flesh.
2. I did not hear the telephone ring yesterday because I was taking a shower, but I got the message in time to go to the party.
3. Although an oncoming bus crowded a truckload of laborers off the road when the two ambulances tore by, nobody got hurt.
4. Because Jean Henri Dunant, a citizen of Switzerland, felt sorry for Austrian soldiers wounded in the Napoleonic Wars, he started an organization, which was later named the Red Cross.
5. Stressing career education, the administrators not only required back-to-basics courses but also kept students informed about job opportunities.

■ **Exercise 4** (pp. 298–99)   **Combining choppy sentences; tightening loose sentences**

1. As I was walking across the campus, I found a twenty-dollar bill.
2. This idea struck me when I was musing on the pleasures of loafing: complete idleness is hard work.
3. Growth stops because insects eat the plant off just below the soil.
4. The little boy, unconscious of our worries and fears, slept through it all.
5. I didn't tell anybody that I felt bad because I didn't want to go to the hospital again.

6. As the yearbook had predicted, within a year the twins married twins.
7. Although the price of peace may be high, the price of war is higher.
8. An intention is not the deed, nor is a blueprint a home.
9. The optimist believes that the battle is worth fighting and that success is inevitable.
10. Oliver, a bantam boxer who likes to throw his weight around, keeps on picking fights.

25 Coherence

It is not enough to collect words, capitalize the first one, place a period after the last one, and call the result a sentence. While students would readily agree that *Boldly dog cat the hissed at* is ungrammatical, they have more difficulty with dangling constructions because the words follow English syntax. The misplaced or dangling parts and the related part(s) are themselves grammatical. The logical bridge (whether a word or word order), however, is not. Yet since students are satisfied with the meaning they derive (in a sentence like *It only costs fifty dollars*) or since they supply the bridge, perhaps without realizing they are doing so (in a sentence like *Walking through the house, clutter greeted her everywhere,* which produces two ideas: *She was walking through the house* and *Clutter greeted her everywhere*), they do not recognize the flaw.

Since a writer cannot depend on readers either to be satisfied or to supply the logical connection, the writer must create coherent sentences. Not doing so risks the reader's laughter as the word order calls up comical, outlandish, or outrageous images that detract from the main idea. Students find the sentences in dangling-modifier exercises laughable; you might point out that those dangling modifiers in students' papers are no less laughable.

ACTIVITIES

1. Ask students to discuss the differences in meaning:

a. 1. Only Jamie said that the novel was inspiring.
   2. Jamie only said that the novel was inspiring.

   3. Jamie said only that the novel was inspiring.
   4. Jamie said that only the novel was inspiring.
   5. Jamie said that the only novel was inspiring.
   6. Jamie said that the novel was only inspiring.

b. 1. Almost everyone was in tears.
   2. Everyone was almost in tears.

c. 1. Merely sweeping the floor once a week is satisfactory.
   2. Sweeping merely the floor once a week is satisfactory.
   3. Sweeping the floor merely once a week is satisfactory.
   4. Sweeping the floor once a week is merely satisfactory.

2. Ask students to revise each sentence, eliminating ''squinting'' modifiers and split infinitives.

   a. Chewing gum slowly calms his nerves.
   b. To entirely remove gum from a shag rug requires patiently scraping gum that has been rubbed with an ice cube repeatedly.
   c. Scraping often takes more patience than I have.
   d. Let's remember to have always guaranteed gum remover just in case we have this problem again.

3. Have students identify the absolute phrases, sentence modifiers, and dangling modifiers in these sentences.

   a. Entering the discussion of favorite authors, Jane Austen and Kurt Vonnegut were mentioned first.   [DM]
   b. The conversation having been prompted by Rachel's enthusiasm for Flannery O'Connor's writing, we began to compile a list of favorite female authors.   [AP]
   c. Speaking of contemporary fiction, who has read Gail Godwin's novels?   [SM]
   d. Kevin suggested the stories of Elizabeth Bowen saying that Caroline Gordon's stories were also some of his favorites.   [DM]
   e. Considering the number of books published every year, I would like to read two or three a week.   [SM]
   f. Feeling fortunate to read two or three a month, the number of must-read books grows faster than I can keep up with.   [DM]
   g. Fiction being put aside for now, my next project is to read every book on the nonfiction best-seller list.   [AP]

4. Ask students to rewrite the sentences from one paragraph of a recent theme by using absolute phrases, sentence modifiers, and elliptical adverbial clauses.

ANSWERS TO EXERCISES

■ **Exercise 1** (pp. 301–02)   **Placing single-word modifiers correctly**

1. killed *only* one student
2. looked *almost* like new
3. cost *nearly* fifty dollars
4. works *even* during his vacation
5. show *hardly* any interest
6. ate *almost* all
7. had *barely* enough

■ **Exercise 2** (p. 302)   **Bringing related parts together**

1. Newspapers in every part of the country
2. date muffins with pecans in them
3. sundaes in paper cups
4. On Monday the professor made it clear

■ **Exercise 3** (pp. 303–04)   **Eliminating squinting modifiers or needless separation of related parts**

1. An official warned the hunter not to carry a loaded rifle in the car.
2. Selby said he would go in the evening. OR In the evening Selby said he would go.
3. Even during the 6:15 P.M. sports news, Marvin wanted to finish our game of checkers.
4. Harriet promised to stop at the library on her way home.
5. The car advertised in last night's paper is only two years old and is in excellent condition.

■ **Exercise 4** (p. 306)   **Eliminating dangling modifiers**

Answers may vary somewhat.

1. While I was wondering about this phenomenon, the sun sank from view.
2. We ended the meeting by standing and repeating the pledge.
3. Once made, the decision must be promptly executed.
4. Prepare to make an incision in the abdomen as soon as the patient is completely anesthetized.
5. After we had sat there awhile, it began to snow, and we went indoors.
6. CORRECT
7. After the witness had taken his seat, we began to question him.

8. Just as we were ready to pitch camp, the windstorm hit.
9. CORRECT
10. Because their house had burned to the ground, the Welches had to build a new one.

■ **Exercise 5** (p. 307)   **Using introductory parenthetical elements to combine sentences**

Answers may vary somewhat.

1. Having a broken arm and nose, the statue is, I think, an interesting antique.
2. When worried about the world situation, James sometimes thought it would be a good idea to join the Peace Corps.
3. After reading the first three questions, I realized that the test covered materials that I had not studied.
4. Only twelve years old, Larry had inventive abilities that his teachers noticed.
5. Turning on the flashers and lifting the hood, I thought that a passing motorist might see my predicament, slow down, and offer me a ride.

26   Parallelism

Like subordination, parallelism is evidence of a writer's ability to express relationships between ideas. By placing comparable ideas in constructions that correspond to each other, the writer uses structure to emphasize content. The similarity of ideas is heightened by their parallel arrangement. In English some parallel constructions occur so frequently that they may not be recognized as such (for example, compound subjects and objects, coordinate adjectives), but others call attention to themselves through the deliberate repetition of lengthy structures or the use of signal words (such as *not only . . . but also*). Parallelism may emphasize similar or opposite ideas; it may—by arranging the parallel items in climactic order—emphasize not only the items but also their degrees of importance. Yet writers who rely on parallelism as their only means of emphasis neglect a variety of other techniques and those who use it excessively create monotonous prose.

ACTIVITIES

1. Ask students to write down a series of parallel sentences begin-ning with *I know that*. Although students begin with the obvious (*I know that today is Tuesday. I know that tomorrow is Wednesday*), as a rule they move on to more reflective thoughts. In any event, they are practicing parallel forms in addition to characterizing themselves by the pieces of information they choose to include. Such constructions as *To _____ is to _____* or *I remember when _____* may also be used.

2. Ask students to write a six-sentence paragraph using at least one set of parallel elements in every sentence. Then have students revise the paragraph, saving only the most effective parallel con-structions.

3. Ask students to write one sentence containing coordinate nouns, verbs, infinitive phrases, participial phrases, and dependent clauses (*Wearing cowboy gear and swaggering through the crowd to advertise the rodeo and to promote Laramie Days, the father and son laughed and whooped as they greeted visitors and even while they sold tickets.*). Have students label each coordinate pair or revise the sentence if any element is missing.

ANSWERS TO EXERCISES

■ **Exercise 1** (pp. 309–10)   **Underlining parallel structures**

1. situations, moods, and relationships
2. America without baseball, Europe without soccer, England with-out cricket, the Italians without bocci, China without Ping-Pong, and tennis for no one
3. To say that some truths are simple . . . to say they are unimpor-tant
4. Reading through *The Origin* . . . eating Cracker Jacks and finding an I O U note
5. mountains taller than Everest, valleys deeper than the Dead Sea rift, and highlands bigger than Australia
6. completed her page, ornamented the foot, threw over the release, spun the roller, flung the carbons, shuffled the copies, slapped them, and bounced

7. who do not need flowers, who cannot be surprised by joy
8. those who are toiled to death, those who are worried to death, and those who are bored to death
9. Booms attract an oversupply, busts generate an undersupply.
10. Not for thirty years has, Not in all this time has, of misunderstanding, of suspicion, of bewilderment, and of sheer military fear.

■ **Exercise 2** (p. 311)   **Inserting words needed for parallel structure**

1. *a* day OR *for a* day
2. *to* succeed
3. *that* I had reasons
4. *by* worrying
5. *an* elephant OR *of an* elephant

■ **Exercise 3** (pp. 312–13)   **Using parallel structures for parallel ideas**

1. It is a rare disease, and it is hard to diagnose.
2. to play tennis and *to watch* basketball
3. both heredity and *environment*
4. CORRECT
5. that the trip would be delayed but *that I should be ready to start on Friday*
6. with the best intentions and *the highest principles*
7. *how* his fellows act and how they obey their trainer
8. quiet and *serious*
9. CORRECT
10. the workers and *the dependents*

27   Shifts

Coherent prose—writing that is consistent, orderly, and logical—usually includes shifts made necessary by the content: the mood of verbs changes from indicative to subjunctive as the writer distinguishes a fact from a condition contrary to fact; direct discourse alternates with indirect discourse to indicate shifts from speech to thought. Such shifts are needed because they help develop the writer's message.

    Some shifts, however, produce inconsistencies that destroy coherence by sending out conflicting information about the relationship of ideas. In the first pair of sentences in 27a, for example, the shift of tenses from *complained* to *discusses* conflicts with words showing that the activities are simultaneous (*during, while*). In the second example the shift from subjunctive to indicative not only signals an illogical condition but also weakens the parallel structure. Such shifts as these obscure the meaning and interfere with coherence.

ACTIVITIES

1. Ask students to identify the needless shifts in the following sentences:

   a. If I was poor and you were rich, would we still be friends?
   b. David has been nominated to fill the vacancy, and almost everyone agrees he would be a conscientious chairman.
   c. One should practice daily if you want to be a concert violinist.
   d. Those who have done our best should never be apologetic.

2. Have students write a paragraph alternating the direct discourse of two speakers and the indirect discourse of a third person.

3. Bring to class copies of one or two student paragraphs and ask students to correct any needless shifts and to justify the others. Or ask students to justify the shifts they find in a professionally written essay.

ANSWERS TO EXERCISES

■ **Exercise 1** (pp. 315–16)   **Correcting needless shifts**

Answers may vary somewhat.

1. asked
2. and that the money be spent
3. he baked it for fifteen minutes
4. All bystanders were
5. that *one* should bathe

■ **Exercise 2** (pp. 317–18)   **Correcting needless shifts**

1. grabbed . . . snatched
2. All enjoy a vacation

3. CORRECT
4. and whether he had said when he would return.
5. All cooks have
6. there was
7. CORRECT but *him* OR *her* OR *him/her* is often preferred
8. You will need it. OR It will be needed.
9. fortress; inside, the
10. to fall asleep

■ **Exercise 3** (p. 318)   **Eliminating needless shifts**

Answers will vary. The following are possibilities.

[1]He is a shrewd businessman, or so it has always seemed to me. [2]He has innocent-looking eyes, which are in a baby face, and swaggers when he walks. [3]When questioned about his recent windfall, he says, "I'm lucky enough to have the right contacts." [4]Not one name does he mention; moreover, he is reluctant to discuss his business transactions. [5]These comments should be taken for what they are worth. They may help one who deals with this shrewd businessman.

28   Reference of Pronouns

The clarity of pronoun-antecedent references depends not only on agreement in person and number but also on the proximity of a specific, expressed antecedent for the pronoun. Thus, broad reference or intervening words may create ambiguity or obscurity that interferes with the reader's understanding of ideas. Although experienced writers may occasionally use broad reference, it rarely increases clarity and precision, so students would profit more by concentrating on the constructions that do.

Every writer, on the other hand, must recognize the different meanings of *it* in order to avoid confusing the reader. To change meanings when repeating a word within a sentence violates the reader's one-word–one-meaning expectation. Thus, these various meanings of *it* should not be placed near each other:

1. *it* as pronoun (*I read the book as soon as I bought it.*)
2. *it* as an expletive (*It is not surprising that he won a scholarship. It is impossible for them to sing on key.*)
3. *it* as an indefinite in expression of time or weather (*It is raining. It is noon.*)

4. *it* as an indefinite in the *it* + noun + *who* or *that* construction
(*It is Larry who suggested a scholarship to honor Professor Williams.*)
5. *it* as a word (*One of the original forms of it was hit.*)

ACTIVITIES

1. Ask students to revise each sentence in three ways: by repeating the antecedent, by using a synonym, and by recasting the sentence.

   a. When four-year-old Cory and two-year-old Brad play together, he always knocks down the blocks.
   b. Our daughter prefers looking through her microscope to cleaning her room. This takes up at least two hours every Saturday morning.
   c. As Greg and his uncle shook hands, he thanked him for the helmet and jersey.

2. Ask students to eliminate the broad reference in each of the following:

   a. They accepted our challenge to play softball once a week. This means we'll have to practice seriously if we expect to win.
   b. Her research paper was written, her finals had been canceled, and her aunt had sent her one hundred dollars. That was not the case for her roommate.

3. Have students revise each sentence to eliminate ambiguous, remote, or obscure references.

   a. If you say it, then it's true that he practices the piano ten hours a day.
   b. It's seven-thirty and it's still raining, but it will pass soon.
   c. Buy them a damask tablecloth or sew them some calico napkins and placemats. It won't matter because they are both nice.
   d. It's a fact that it hasn't been the same since Mary left.
   e. Because Chris had budgeted wisely, it meant he could buy a new tape deck. Which he had been looking forward to for more than a year.

4. Select two or three letters from an advice column and have students identify the antecedent for each pronoun. Have students use pronouns in writing an answer to one letter not discussed in class.

ANSWERS TO EXERCISES

■ **Exercise 1** (pp. 321–22)   **Eliminating ambiguous, remote, or obscure reference**

Answers may vary. The following are possibilities.

1. The misunderstanding between the two families did not end until the Kemps invited the Dixons over for a swim in their new pool.
2. buttons and knobs that are clearly labeled seldom cause confusion
3. After Martin had launched his advertising campaign, he
4. acres. It is well stocked with fish. Near the shore
5. As Elaine was coming down the ramp, she waved to Mrs. Edwards.

■ **Exercise 2** (p. 324)   **Correcting faulty reference of pronouns**

Answers may vary. The following are possibilities.

1. but chow mein is their favorite food.
2. water leaked all over the kitchen floor
3. assistants can manage these machines easily and quickly.
4. The book states that
5. CORRECT
6. My failure even to buy a season ticket was very disloyal to my school.
7. "I have to read *Shogun*," Mary told Ann.
8. might cover the roads and make them useless.
9. Extra fees that seemed unreasonably high surprised many freshmen.
10. Frank packs only wash-and-wear clothes in his suitcase.

29   Emphasis

Writers achieve emphasis by deciding which ideas are most important and arranging them for greatest effect. Students who practice the eight techniques in Section 29 will gain in the power to influence their audience through the emphasis of ideas.

Once students have decided which ideas are most important and why, they are ready to try out these techniques—one at a time or in combination—until they find the most effective one for each idea. Experimenting with the options, students eventually come to rely on three or four with which they feel most comfortable; they should be encouraged to use other techniques occasionally, too. Finally, students should look at each sentence in the context of the paragraph to determine whether any technique is ineffective or overused; if so, revision is called for.

You might discuss with students which methods they are most likely to notice and why. Such methods as using active voice and arranging ideas in order of climax may not be associated with emphasis, while periodic and balanced sentences may be. Although the latter are characteristic of formal writing, students should not think that emphasis and formality are synonymous.

ACTIVITIES

1. Have students select four sentences from a paragraph of their favorite theme. Ask students to rewrite the sentences using each of the eight techniques in Section 29 for each of the sentences and to devise some simple tabular arrangement that will allow them to compare the resulting sentences. Students will see that they may have already used some techniques and that not all methods suit every sentence.

   For each of the original sentences, have students select the revision they find most effective. Ask students which methods they are most comfortable with. Have students put their favorite revised sentences into a paragraph and make any changes necessary for ease of reading.

2. Have students use another paragraph which they enjoyed writing or which they think is particularly effective. Ask them to rewrite the paragraph using any three of the eight emphasis techniques. Once they finish, ask them to label each use. Then have them rewrite the paragraph using three of the remaining five methods. Ask them which paragraph they prefer. The goal here is not to achieve flawless arrangements but to explore the possible combinations; the discovery of combinations that do not work well together is just as valuable as the discovery of those that do.

3. Have groups of students write a paragraph consisting of one topic sentence, one or two sentences of support, one or two sentences of examples, and a concluding sentence. All sentences should be

in subject-verb-object order, in active voice, in loose rather than periodic structure, and of approximately equal length. Ask groups of students to exchange and rewrite paragraphs.

4. Have students analyze one body paragraph from a recent theme by answering these questions:

   a. How many sentences does the paragraph contain?
   b. How many words does each sentence contain? What is the average number of words per sentence?
   c. In which sentences are important words at the beginning or end?
   d. Which sentences are loose?
   e. Which sentences use the order of climax?
   f. Which sentences use active voice?
   g. What are the one or two most important words? How often is each word repeated?
   h. Not counting dangling modifiers, how many times are words emphasized by being out of usual order? Which sentences are inverted? How many of the inverted sentences are questions?
   i. Which sentences are balanced?

   After students answer these questions, ask them to list conclusions drawn from the analysis. Have them write a paragraph describing their methods of emphasis and suggesting one way to improve their arrangement of ideas.

5. Ask students to analyze one paragraph from a published essay.

ANSWERS TO EXERCISES

■ **Exercise 1** (pp. 326–27) **Revising for emphasis**

Answers will vary. The following are possibilities.

1. Music has the power to hypnotize.
2. Only one person could have written all these articles because of their same political slant.
3. One stunt woman earns five thousand dollars for two hours of work.
4. Lewisville finally decided to enforce the old ordinance; nearby towns revived similar laws and also began clean-up campaigns.

5. Never before had it entered her mind to resent her husband's complacent ignorance or to ignore his unreasonable demands.

■ **Exercise 2** (p. 328)   **Converting loose sentences into periodic, periodic into loose**

Answers may vary somewhat. The following are possibilities.

1. Despite everything, Italy remains cheerful.
2. Old habits and reflexes persist, even where people want better relations.
3. The Milky Way Galaxy, one of billions of other galaxies strewn through the vastness of space, is entirely unremarkable.
4. Nervously backing away from the arguments she should have had with my father, turning aside from the talks she should have had with me, she was then (as always, as she had been all her life) sweet and apologetic.
5. "I just oppose it if I don't know anything about something, or if I don't understand it," Mays told me, almost with pride.

■ **Exercise 3** (p. 330)   **Arranging ideas in order of climax**

Answers may vary somewhat. The following are possibilities.

1. industry, efficiency, and wisdom
2. sun-drenched orchards, golden-flecked birds, and diamond-eyed children
3. his pet dog was tired of the leash, his taxes were going up, and his health was failing
4. The commission is faced with a deficit. Something must be done at once. Unless we act now, the city will be bankrupt in five years.
5. autographed books for teenagers, wrote letters to senior citizens, attended a community festival, and promised prosperity to all.

■ **Exercise 4** (pp. 330–31)   **Substituting the active for the passive voice**

1. Tourists often throw pennies into the fountain.
2. Every Saturday morning, easily influenced children watch television.
3. A student about to run out of coins was filling the wastebasket with illegible photocopies.
4. When the play ended, the audience greeted the actors with a loud burst of applause.
5. The citizens greatly fear that the judge will not mete out adequate punishment.

■ **Exercise 5** (p. 331)   **Using repetition instead of synonyms**

1. Sometimes we lie . . . ; sometimes we lie
2. . . . he gripes about the weather, gripes about heavy traffic, gripes about high prices, and gripes about his meals.

■ **Exercise 9** (p. 334)   **Revising for emphasis**

Answers will vary. The following are possibilities.

1. Experimenting on fetuses, whether they are dead or alive, should stop.
2. These retirees fear poverty, illness, death.
3. All around us were fields of wild flowers.
4. Fools talk about each other; wise people talk about ideas.
5. When the fleeing youth tripped over the patrolman's foot, the gun fired.
6. At the close of a hot day, the storm broke in all its fury.
7. Milburn caught a fast pass and gained thirty yards before the referee blew the whistle.
8. Two years ago, late in the fall, in a shop on Tremont Street, I asked her to marry me.
9. Although their art was crude, some of the people showed a great deal of originality.
10. By the simple device of choosing the least likely suspect whose alibi is airtight, I can identify the guilty person in every Agatha Christie novel.

30 Variety

Emphasis is the arrangement of ideas in a sentence to highlight their relative importance. Variety is the arrangement of sentences to create changes in both structure and length that keep the reader's attention on the flow of ideas. Since most students begin their sentences with the subject and give little or no thought to the length of their sentences, varying length and sentence beginnings are the first topics to discuss.

Sentence lengths do not vary according to some arbitrary rule, such as twenty words, eight words, twelve words, two longs, a short, and a long. Lengths do vary according to the kinds of information presented: explanations, illustrations, and other supporting material tend to require longer sentences than topic sentences or transitions.

Adequate development involves more qualifications of and relationships among ideas than are contained in a topic sentence. But not all supporting sentences are long—an abrupt change in length may be used for emphasis. And not all topic sentences are short—they may include a transition in addition to the several ideas directing the paragraph. Variation for its own sake is ineffective; the goal is variation that attends to the needs of both the ideas and the audience.

In addition to the suggestions in 30b for varying sentence beginnings, you might use these patterns:

1. an infinitive or infinitive phrase (*To cut the logs into firewood, he used a chain saw.*)
2. an introductory series (*The porcelain vase, the hand-painted platter, and the domed butter dish—these the movers packed in a special carton.*)
3. a noun clause as either subject or direct object (*That they kept their promise pleases me.*)

ACTIVITIES

1. Have students write a paragraph of five or six sentences, each beginning with the subject and each consisting of twelve to fifteen words. Ask students to rewrite the paragraph, varying both sentence lengths and beginnings. Have students exchange papers and revise the original paragraph. Ask students to discuss the merits of each revised paragraph. (If class size prevents a whole-group discussion of all the paragraphs, divide students into groups of three and proceed as above.)

2. Have students analyze one paragraph from the first theme of the semester and one from the most recent theme by answering these questions for each:

   a. How many words does each sentence contain? What is the longest sentence? Why? (complexity of ideas, wordiness, etc.) What is the shortest sentence? Why? Where does it occur? (beginning, middle, end)
   b. Which sentences are declarative? interrogative? imperative? exclamatory?
   c. Which sentences begin with the subject? a sentence connective? an adverb? an adverb clause? a prepositional phrase? a

participial phrase? an infinitive? an infinitive phrase? an appositive? an absolute? a series? a noun clause?

d. Which sentences are simple? compound? complex? compound-complex?

e. In which sentences do words intervene between the subject
and verb?

Asking students *which* sentences, instead of merely how many,
requires them to look closely at patterns and to discover whether
the variety, if any, is confined to one section of the paragraph or is
evenly distributed throughout. Have students describe their findings by writing a one-paragraph summary for each paragraph analyzed.

3. Have students choose three ways of varying sentence structure
and include them in the revision of one paragraph from a recent
theme. Then have students revise the original paragraph again by
using three different methods.

4. Ask students to prepare to discuss Exercises 3 and 7 (or paragraphs they have collected) by answering the questions used to
analyze their own prose.

ANSWERS TO EXERCISES

■ **Exercise 2** (pp. 337–38) **Combining sentences to relate ideas**

Answers will vary. The following are possibilities.

1. With thirty seconds of play left, Harrison intercepted the pass,
raced downfield, and dropped the ball at the five-yard line.

2. Her speech had an interesting thesis: salespersons should not only
solve the existing problems of their customers but should also
point out new problems in order to solve them.

3. Bennett's Comet, which appeared in 1969 and disappeared in
1970, will not be visible again for thousands of years.

4. Instead of buying a second car, Ellen Dolan bought a Piper, a cub
plane, which flies at almost a hundred miles an hour.

5. In his book *Kinship with All Life,* J. Allen Boone describes his
ability to communicate with animals; he converses mentally with a
dog; he orders ants to leave his home, and they obey; he even
tames an ordinary housefly.

■ **Exercise 4** (pp. 340–41)   **Recasting sentences to vary the beginnings**

Answers will vary. The following are possibilities.

1. a. Between the members of our sororities and fraternities, we still need a better understanding.
   b. Still we need a better understanding between the members of our sororities and fraternities.
2. a. Interviewing the newly appointed ambassador, reporters asked him some tricky questions about world affairs.
   b. In their interview with the newly appointed ambassador, reporters asked him some tricky questions about world affairs.
3. a. Lining up in order to register in a floating university, the *Queen Victoria,* were hundreds of students.
   b. In order to register in a floating university, the *Queen Victoria,* hundreds of students lined up.
4. a. Most of all, Jesse enjoyed the course in science-fiction literature.
   b. The course in science-fiction literature Jesse enjoyed most of all.
5. a. Traveling at great speed, the green fireballs fascinated sky watchers throughout the Southwest.
   b. Fascinating sky watchers throughout the Southwest, the green fireballs traveled at great speed.

■ **Exercise 5** (p. 342)   **Revising loose, stringy compound sentences**

Answers will vary. The following are possibilities.

1. Even though the small car hugs the road and is easy to drive in traffic, it is not comfortable.
2. Growing tired of city smog and noise pollution, the Johnsons moved to the country, where they had no fire department or police protection.
3. After first trading their products and then using money and bank checks, Americans now use the all-inclusive plastic credit card.
4. Mentioning such things as marriage and two-car garages, Harvey kept criticizing middle-class values, but he did not define upper-class or lower-class values.

■ **Exercise 6** (p. 343)   **Varying subject-verb sequence**

Answers will vary. The following are possibilities.

1. Roger, like his mother, is an excellent conversationalist.

2. Rhode Island, east of Connecticut, has a forty-mile coastline.
3. My grandparents, valuing strong family ties, encouraged us young ones ''to always keep in touch.''
4. Margaret, racing back to the dormitory to avoid getting wet, fell broadside into a big puddle of water.
5. Wizzard Wells, a popular resort once, is a ghost town now.

31 The Paragraph

Unity, coherence, and development—all depend on the topic sentence. For that reason, students should be able both to identify the topic sentences of others and to write limited, concrete, succinct sentences of their own.

Since a topic sentence controls the development of the entire paragraph, it should be an incisive statement of the main idea. As such, it should contain no signs of weak construction (such as expletives, passive voice, intensifiers such as *really, truly, very*) or of words that depend on another sentence to complete their meaning (such as a personal pronoun). And although students will most often place a topic sentence at the beginning of the paragraph, they should at least practice the other placements.

In explaining how to develop ideas, the instructor might point out that regardless of the pattern(s) used in a paragraph, the basic elements remain topic sentence, explanation or clarification, supporting examples or proof, summary, and transition. Thus, methods of development do not allow the writer to omit any of these basics. In fact, the topic sentence determines the method, which then shapes the explanation and support sections.

ACTIVITIES

1. Using one professionally written paragraph containing a topic sentence, two or three sentences of explanation, one or two sentences of illustration, and a summary sentence, type the sentences in random order. Ask students to identify the function of each sentence. Then have students construct the paragraph by placing the topic sentence at the beginning, in the middle, and at the end, making any changes required by the placement. Ask students

which of the three versions they prefer and why before showing them the original paragraph.

2. Have students revise a body paragraph from a recent theme by placing the topic sentence at the beginning, in the middle, and at the end. **Note:** a paragraph of contrast or of example lends itself well to this exercise because the parts are readily identified and rearranged.

3. Ask students to select one or two paragraphs from a textbook, to identify the topic sentence and the pattern of development.

4. Have students collect paragraphs to illustrate the various patterns of development. Ask them to underline the topic sentence of each paragraph.

5. Ask students to evaluate the unity of one of their paragraphs by justifying the function of every sentence in the paragraph.

6. Select one topic sentence from each student's theme (include specific as well as general ones). Have students revise general sentences. Ask them what question(s) implied in the topic sentence must be answered in the development of the paragraph.

7. Ask students to create titles for eight essays they would like to write if time, skill, and knowledge were unlimited. Each of the eight titles should imply one of the categories of paragraph development.

8. Have students collect examples of different strategies for opening paragraphs (quotation, rhetorical question, anecdote, example, statistics, or a combination of these) and then rewrite one of the opening paragraphs using a different strategy or combination of strategies.

9. Bring to class copies of two or three student paragraphs. In each, label the ways unity is gained (by pronouns, key words, transitions, or parallel structure). Then ask students to analyze a paragraph they have written recently and revise it to improve unity.

10. Have students analyze one of their essays to discover which categories of transitions are most frequently used and which, if any, are not used or are used infrequently. Have students share their

analyses with the class. Ask students to compare their use of unifying strategies with those of a professional writer.

11. To demonstrate that description is based on observation and that powers of observation vary, during the final fifteen minutes of class burn a scented pillar candle—one that has been used several times before so that it will have an interesting shape. Have students describe the candle (ask them to write a list of fifty observations, but settle for twenty-five or so). Before the next class, type up the observations paragraph-style to save space. Ask students to compare the differences, thus opening a discussion of perception or of objective and subjective description.

12. To emphasize the use of criteria in classifying objects into parallel, nonoverlapping categories, bring to class an apparently random assortment of silverware (knives, forks, teaspoons, sugar spoons, serving spoons, pickle forks, steak knives, stainless, silverplate, plastic, etc.). Ask students to group items according to function, material, pattern, finish.

13. Review methods of paragraph development by analyzing essay examination questions from various fields (such as psychology, textiles, child development, nursing, physics, literature, music, engineering). Explain that regardless of students' knowledge of the subject, they can structure an answer. Ask them first to identify the type(s) of development implied by the questions and then to outline how they would proceed to answer the question. (Colleagues may be willing to share questions, or instructors may devise their own.) This exercise also provides an opportunity to discuss how to write an essay exam and how to cope with insufficiently clear and specific questions.

ANSWERS TO EXERCISES

■ **Exercise 2** (p. 351–52)   **Identifying topic sentences**

Paragraph 6: first sentence
Paragraph 7: first sentence
Paragraph 8: Implied, as is often the case in a description. The following might be supplied: *Here is a description of the living room* or *The living room looked like this.*

■ **Exercise 3** (pp. 354–55)   Identifying paragraph patterns

Paragraph 12: Question-answer
Paragraph 13: Topic-illustration
Paragraph 14: Topic-Restriction (the phrase beginning "after")-Illustration. (Note that the last sentence of the paragraph restates the first.)
Paragraph 15: Topic-Restriction (burning of fossil fuel)-Illustration. (A possible alternative is Problem-Solution. Though the paragraph offers no solution, it does stress the need for one.)

■ **Exercise 4** (p. 363)   Identifying patterns and development methods

Paragraph 27: Pattern: Topic-Illustration, developed by examples and comparison
Paragraph 28: Pattern: Topic-Illustration, developed by classification
Paragraph 29: Pattern: Topic-Illustration, developed by examples

■ **Exercise 5** (p. 365)   Revising a paragraph

Answers will vary. When you assign this exercise, you may want to suggest a paragraph pattern. Topic-Restriction-Illustration (in that order) works well here:

> Topic: the need to control a hostile environment
> Restriction: the unforeseen result of destroying the environment by controlling it
> Illustrations: pollution, scarcity of resources

You may also want to suggest that the students retain the chronological method of development, as it works well.

■ **Exercise 6** (p. 370)   Identifying linking devices

Paragraph 41 contains the following linking devices:

> pronouns: *it* for *electronic music* (used three times)
> transitional words: *also*
> repetition: *music, electric(ally), sound(s)*
> parallelism: *It is the product* . . .
>   *It is the sounds* . . .

■ **Exercise 7** (p. 370)   Revising sentences

Answers will vary. Here is a possible revision:

> When we hear the word "environment," one of the first things

that comes to mind is the weather. While we have created an artificial environment which can be either hot or cool to suit our needs, we cannot create a natural environment because there is no substitute for the sun. While we depend on the sun for heat, it is possible to produce heat artificially. But we also depend on the sun for ultraviolet radiation, which forms the vitamin D in our bodies. The sun is the catalyst which continues our never-ending food chain. Without the sun we could not survive.

Even after this revision, the paragraph reveals fundamental problems that remain unresolved—for example, vitamin D can be chemically synthesized. What the student writer really seems to want to say is that our world would be cold and dark without the sun; hence the sun is essential to life.

■ **Exercise 8** (p. 375)   **Revising a paragraph**

Paragraph 48 lacks an explicitly stated topic sentence, such as *Sometimes being helpful can hurt a good Samaritan.*

■ **Exercise 9** (pp. 375–77)   **Paragraphing an essay**

Various divisions can be made in the essay. In the scheme below, each sentence marks a distinct time break over the eighteen-year period and thus serves as a topic-sentence equivalent in controlling the content of each paragraph:

Paragraph 2: Ronnie A. Ward, born July 10, 1949 . . .
           3: The first time I met Ronnie . . .
           4: When Ronnie was sixteen . . .
           5: When Ronnie turned eighteen . . .
           6: The next time I saw Ronnie . . .
           7: September 14, 1967, started out . . .
           8: At dusk our unit . . .

32   The Whole Composition

The various stages of the student essay in this section demonstrate several common beginners' errors: composing a thesis statement only to ignore it, using weak verbs in topic sentences, failing to recognize the proper sequence of ideas, using general examples, creating an overly long introduction, emphasizing proofreading at the expense of revising. Such errors result from an inability to perceive the essay as a whole or a failure to define and revise ideas with the audience in mind.

In this section, then, the emphasis should be on writing as a process and revising as a critically important part of that process. Although the rules state what seems to be the obvious, students who heretofore have considered only the product of writing may examine their own composing habits in light of the steps presented here. The rules focus on the importance of pre-writing (students should not equate spontaneous or free writing with essay writing). And the rules stress revision, emphasizing the difference between revising strategies (clarifying, restructuring, deleting, or adding ideas as meanings emerge) and proofreading (correcting errors in spelling, mechanics, punctuation, and grammar). Since one hallmark of an experienced writer is the ability to revise for clarity of ideas (rather than revising individual words by simply substituting, omitting, or adding words), students need to work toward that goal.

The parts of the process are, of course, interdependent, but shaping the thesis statement deserves particular attention. As the fulcrum on which the essay balances, the thesis indicates what has gone before and points to what should follow. By discussing the content, diction, and structure of the thesis statement, you can easily show how the same principles transfer to the essay itself.

Further, while professional writers may use a fragment, a rhetorical question, or a series of sentences to convey the controlling idea, a beginning writer benefits from the discipline of composing a single sentence that identifies the organizational pattern to be used in developing the main idea. As soon as students master the one-sentence form, they may wish to consider one of the others.

ACTIVITIES

1. After students have written an essay, ask them to list in chronological order and in as much detail as possible all of the steps that they went through as they wrote. Use their lists to introduce the concept of writing as a process: Which part of the process is the most difficult? Which is the easiest? Which are students most likely to rush through?

2. Ask students how they think professional writers differ from them in work habits, interests, and background.

3. Ask students whether there is any truth in the following statements:

   a. Good writing is spontaneous and natural.
   b. The essay is a form of writing that is not used much any more.
   c. Essays are usually equated with dull information.
   d. Students' essays should be written to please the instructor.
   e. As long as the ideas are clear, grammar and spelling are relatively unimportant.

4. Have students write on the board their thesis statements for the next theme. Analyze every statement for clarity and adequately narrowed subject. Ask students what the strengths and weaknesses of each statement are and have them suggest improvements. Ask students to submit a revised thesis at the next class meeting.

5. Have students compare articles on the same or similar topics written for a specialized and for a general audience. They might, for example, select an article from a professional journal in their field and then look for a comparable topic in a popular magazine. If they are unfamiliar with appropriate journals, have them ask their instructors.

6. Ask students to underline the thesis statement and the topic sentences in their themes. Then ask students working in groups of two or three to evaluate the clarity of the sentences and development of ideas.

7. Type up the first sentence from each student's introduction. Discuss the effectiveness of the sentences in gaining the attention of the audience.

8. After students have completed an essay, ask them to write a sentence outline of it as a way to check the sequence and importance of ideas.

9. Have students exchange thesis statements and write an outline of what the thesis indicates will be in the essay.

10. Ask students to select the one subject they know best and to use list-making, the journalist's questions, and the purposes of writing to derive a minimum of twenty different topics.

11. Ask students to share hints to reduce the stress and anxiety often associated with writing. See, for example, "How to Cope With the Stress of Writing" by Tom Mach (*Writer's Digest,* July 1981, pages 22–28) for some suggestions offered to professional writers.

ANSWERS TO EXERCISES

■ **Exercise 1** (pp. 381–83)   **Determining kinds of writing**

The essay is mainly expository. In paragraph 1 the authors introduce their definition of *preservation* with a definition of what preservation is *not:* "What they [people] have done to a building or area of a certain age," which is actually a type of demolition (paragraph 2). The literal definition (paragraph 3) is extended to include maintenance (paragraph 4), and examples of preservation according to that definition fill paragraph 5. The essay is secondarily argumentative to convince readers that preservation-maintenance is worthwhile and that " 'preservation-ists' " misunderstandings result in demolition.

■ **Exercise 4** (p. 392)   **Identifying unrelated material**

Answers will vary. Here are some possibilities:

1. All but vacuuming and dusting are security measures. Or, mowing the lawn may be necessary while vacationers are away, but the other tasks should be done before they leave on vacation.
2. The first two are methods of developing a definition (contrast, illustration) while the third simply shows some of the essays that have been written.
3. The second and the third items could be used to describe how budgeting affects the writer's emotions; a definition of money does not.

■ **Exercise 6** (p. 395)   **Revising thesis statements**

Answers will vary, but asking students to consider questions raised by the thesis statements will clarify the kinds of changes necessary.

1. How are the sports different? (equipment, number of players, score keeping, offensive and defensive strategies)
2. What was the job? What were its duties or responsibilities? How does "do anything as well as a man" apply specifically to the summer job?

3. How can photography be interesting if a person knows nothing about it? What facets would a beginner find interesting? Why?
4. What categories of factors: career, emotional, physical? What specific factors in each category?
5. Which car? What are its gas mileage and maintenance costs? How does it compare with similar models?
6. What is a "fun vacation"? What is wilderness camping? How does it differ from other kinds of camping? Who should attempt it? Why does it test campers' ingenuity?

■ **Exercise 8** (p. 397)   **Shaping topics for an audience**

Answers will vary. The following are possibilities.

1. college students—lyrics as social criticism; long-term effects of high decibel levels
   country-western fans—shared features of both kinds of music
   composers—how innovations in recording technology expand composers' options
2. state taxpayers—benefits to the public of current state-funded research; tax credits for tuition; state extension services
   high school seniors—availability of scholarships; variety of offerings
   alumni—building programs; services offered alumni as part of job search
3. city commissioners—need for rigorous enforcement of housing codes
   school administrators—how off-campus housing affects on-campus residence halls
   students—economic advantages of living off-campus
   rental-property owners—how to enforce a lease agreement; legal responsibilities of landlords
4. home gardeners—how to harvest potatoes efficiently
   commercial growers—how to cut costs and increase profits by studying consumer buying habits
   nutritionists—evidence to refute the idea of potatoes as fattening food
5. general audience—changing definition of *family* to include more than the traditional nuclear family; the effect of two-career families or marriages on the economy
   religious groups—marriage ceremonies in non-Christian cultures
   sociologists—what marriage contracts reveal about traditional husband-wife roles; how parents' divorce affects children's view of parenting when they become parents

■ **Exercise 9** (pp. 397–400)   **Considering the audience**

The subject of Sheed's commencement address—intellectual growth—may be a familiar one, and his conviction that reading is the key to intellectual life may be equally familiar (or should be to anyone who has ever sat in an English class, whether writing or literature), but the way he conveys his belief is anything but familiar or conventional. No platitudes, no quotations for graduates to live by—just a witty analysis of the shriveling effect of life without books or new ideas. To begin a discussion of the differences between spoken and written English, students might identify elements of spoken English found here (''people in the same boat,'' ''second-raters,'' ''they made you do it''), comparing them with the elements of formal writing that they would expect in an essay.

■ **Exercise 13** (p. 414)   **Analysis of second draft**

Answers may vary. Points not revised: weak verb in topic sentence (paragraph 2), proof that items were originally high priced (paragraph 1), partial answer to question of security (paragraph 4). Checklist questions that still need attention: 1, 9, 11, 15, 17, 18–25.

■ **Exercise 15** (p. 419)   **Revising the second draft**

Suggestions for revising will vary. Proofreading corrections should include the misused semicolon in paragraph 2, line 11, and the use of *personnel* for *personal* in paragraph 5.

33   The Research Paper

Students often perceive the research paper as altogether different from or more important than their other writing assignments. Instead of recognizing that the same process operates in both—defining, shaping, collecting, and revising—they concentrate on collecting information. For several reasons students may divorce writing a research paper from writing essays:

1. The research paper is longer and more formal than an essay.
2. It is given more class time and more time for writing than any other essay.
3. It requires conventional research format (formal outline, notes, bibliography).

4. It is the type of essay most often required in other classes.
5. It is weighted more heavily in the final grade than any other essay.

With this perception, students tend to fall into the trap of budgeting most of their time for research, relatively little for writing, and almost none for revising. Losing sight of the composing process, the students rely heavily on conventions of format to carry their ideas. You can help students balance their attention to the steps in the process by reviewing each of the rules in Section 32 in terms of the research paper, by helping students to invent subjects, and by allowing time for revision after a conference on the second draft. Thus, by commenting on the entire process and by including time for revision, you can work to eliminate overemphasis of a single aspect.

After planning adequate time for each step, announce the schedule of deadlines for the unit. At the same time, announce your policy on late papers and missed conferences so that students have a clear understanding of what is expected of them from the outset.

Here are a few cautions if you assign works of literature as subjects for a research paper:

1. Do not assume that students possess the skills to read literature critically. They need help to understand a literary work so that their inexperience in interpreting literature does not unfairly hamper their ability to write a good essay.
2. Show them how list-making, the journalist's questions, and the four kinds of writing can be applied to literary terms in order to produce a topic.
3. Place on library reserve copies of the most important articles and books so that students have equal access to them.
4. Select at least three or four works—all, preferably, by different authors—to relieve the strain on the library's resources and to appeal to a variety of interests and reading abilities.
5. To avoid students' relying on *Masterplots* or *Reader's Guide* for their information, you may want to distribute a list of bibliographic resources (with call numbers if possible) for students' use.

Whatever the subject of their research papers, students should be aware that the papers must go beyond simply reporting general information. Unlike high-school research papers, college-level papers require something beyond what is included in encyclopedia entries. Although students may want to read encyclopedias for background information, they are not adequate resources for a research project.

You might suggest that when students take information from a journal or magazine they note on the bibliography card whether the source uses continuous or separate pagination. Thus, the students are prepared to write their endnotes or footnotes in accurate form.

A candid discussion of plagiarism and its penalty informs the student and protects the instructor. In explaining the various kinds, be sure to stress the writer's responsibility for quoting accurately, paraphrasing carefully, and acknowledging honestly all of the sources cited. Students understand that copying sentences verbatim without proper documentation and passing another student's paper off as their own are examples of plagiarism. However, they usually do not know that misrepresenting the facts of publication, paraphrasing without a citation, or duplicating the order of another writer's examples are also examples of plagiarism. Tell the students to bring the original source as well as their use of it to you if they have any doubts about their use of materials. Thus, they can have troublesome summaries or paraphrases evaluated before they write the final draft of their paper.

What, though, about the student who, having been told that his or her paper is plagiarized (containing, for example, more than one series of sentences quoted without acknowledgment) contends that the instructor never discussed it—after the instructor devoted an entire class hour to it? Such protests might be avoided by having all the students sign a form stating that they have heard the discussion of plagiarism, know what it is, and understand the penalty.

As part of the research-paper unit, student-instructor conferences allow you to offer specific suggestions during the writing process, and these conferences benefit both you and the student by focusing on writing. The students prepare for the conference by writing whatever is required, making a list of questions to ask, and arriving on time. You prepare by signing up students for conference times, and by making a checklist of items to comment on. (Since a day of fifteen-minute conferences is exhausting, you should also schedule a break or two.) The students come away satisfied that their papers have been improved; you are reassured that students are writing their own papers.

ACTIVITIES

1. During the first class meeting of the semester include some questions about the students' experience with research papers: how many, if any, they have written; for which courses; on what subjects. When, later in the semester, students select subjects for their research papers, you may choose to disallow areas in which the student has already written a paper.

2. Ask students to write a paraphrase and a précis for one passage you have chosen for the purpose. In a class where the research paper topics cover a number of areas, you might hand out a passage from an article in the area of most of the papers or use a paragraph from the essay anthology used in class. In a class where a literary topic has been assigned, you could choose a passage from a critical work—in a paper on *Nineteen Eighty-Four,* for example, one of the items mentioned in the bibliography for the model research paper in Section **33.** Or, if the students are using a standard sourcebook, such as Irving Howe's *Orwell's* Nineteen Eighty-Four: *Text, Sources, Criticism* (2nd ed., Harcourt, 1982), you could simply ask them to turn to a passage you have chosen.

   Have students write their paraphrases and précis on the board for analysis. Review the rules for the ellipsis mark (**17i**); then ask students to quote the passage directly in a way that requires the ellipsis mark. Have students write their sentence on the board; ask others to make any corrections necessary.

3. Bring to class photocopies of title pages and copyright pages for several books (or reproduce them from an overhead projector). Ask students which information belongs in a bibliographic entry and in what order. Then have them write the entry. (*Note:* Select material carefully to avoid such complications as identifying tags (for example, *former ambassador to the United Nations*), subtitles, and copyright pages with both printing dates and copyright dates.)

4. Ask students to bring to class their preliminary bibliographies, at least six blank 3 × 5-inch cards, and a rubber band or large paper clip. Then select five sources from each student's bibliography, aiming for as much variety as possible—a journal article, a book with two editions, an essay in an anthology, a multivolume work, etc. Each student writes the proper bibliographic form on one side of a card and footnote form on the other. To hand in the cards, students arrange them in proper bibliographical order. Two students using the same source but producing different entries should have an opportunity to compare and correct forms. (**Note:** This exercise has the advantage of testing students' ability to use the forms with sources that they will eventually include in the final bibliography.)

5. Arrange for students to tour the university library. If there is an opportunity to consult with the staff members who conduct the

tours, explain what subjects students have selected and ask that appropriate reference tools be pointed out. Give students a list of questions to ask about library facilities and reference tools. The questions should correlate with students' subjects, and any questions not answered by the librarian's presentation should be asked by someone in the class. These questions might include:

a. What classification system is used for books that circulate?
b. What is the difference between an abstract and an index?
c. Where is the most convenient place to check the call number of a book listed in the *Essay and General Literature Index?*
d. Once I have located an article in an index, where do I look to see whether or not the library has the journal in which it appears?
e. Where is the Minneapolis *Tribune* [or a similar major regional newspaper] index located?
f. What is the library's policy on students' reshelving books?
g. If I know both the author and the title of a book, which card catalog would I go to first and why?

6. Using a student outline from a previous semester, type the sentences in random order. Ask students to reconstruct the outline. The instructor may or may not provide the skeleton of numbers and letters for the outline.

34 Business Writing

While this section is devoted to business letters and resumés, it also provides an opportunity to review all of the elements of clear, effective writing. Letters must accomplish their purpose in relatively few words (usually one typed page or less). Thus, every word must contribute to the message without confusing or offending the reader.

Four of the elements to review include:

1. *Formulating and developing a thesis.* Because "time is money," a business person wants to know immediately why the letter was written and what action, if any, the writer expects. The opening paragraph contains the thesis, which is developed by careful explanation and relevant details in the body paragraphs. The concluding paragraph should state who does what next.

2. *Analyzing an audience.* Here the writer should consider how the addressee will react. Will he or she be pleased by the request (an order for camping gear), irritated (a demand that certain repairs be made to an apartment before the rent is paid), or both (a rush shipment of bayberry candles the week before Christmas)? If the response is likely to be at least in part negative, the writer should organize the letter so that the reader is not overpowered by the negative elements. The tone should be neither insulting nor patronizing.

3. *Diction.* Clear, exact words convey precise images (*a Zenith 19-inch portable color television, model number 194467792,* instead of *my new color television*). Jargon, on the other hand, impresses only those who do not think. Such phrases as *time frame* or *analyzation of invoiced goods as per your aforementioned authorization* are not only imprecise and therefore inefficient, but also boring.

4. *Mechanics and spelling.* Readers of letters and resumés expect standard spelling and mechanics; anything less creates a negative impression. It goes without saying that the addressee's and company's names must be spelled correctly. In letters of application and resumés especially, accuracy is imperative; more resumés are eliminated for reasons of sloppiness and misspelling than for any other.

Students who are applying for jobs should be advised to prepare their resumés before writing letters of application. Writing a resumé should not be a hurried affair. For each of the four major sections students should answer several questions as they collect and organize material:

Personal data

1. How should I give my name (no nicknames)?
2. Is it necessary to include both my school address and my home address? If so, what format should I use?

Suggested Format:

Diane Bellows

Until May 20, 1981	After May 20, 1981
1830 Lexington Avenue	2158 Claussen Trail
Louisville, KY 40227	West Lafayette, IN 47906
(502) 698–3137	(317) 712–8798

Educational background

1. What is the formal name of the school(s) I have attended? (for example, The Pennsylvania State University, not Penn State)
2. What degree(s) did I earn?
3. What are the dates during which I attended?
4. What was my major? minor?
5. What was my grade-point average overall? in my major? in my minor?
6. What advanced seminars or research projects have I taken that are related to the job(s) for which I am applying?
7. What academic honors did I earn?
8. What professional organizations did I join? What offices or committee memberships did I hold? When? What were the responsibilities of each position I held?
9. What social organizations did I join?

Work experience

1. What jobs—including volunteer work—have I held?
2. What were the dates of employment for each job?
3. What was the job title for each position?
4. What was the name of the company for whom I worked?
5. Who was my supervisor or boss?
6. What were my responsibilities?

Location of credentials file

1. What is the official title and address of the Placement Office?
2. What is the telephone number of the Placement Office?
3. Which employers and professors should I ask for letters of recommendation? How many letters should I have in my file?
4. How can I judge who will write the most effective letter?
5. What is the correct procedure for requesting a letter?
6. How soon should I check to see whether my file contains all of the necessary letters?
7. What should I do if a letter has not been sent yet?

After the information has been collected, the student should write each section (obviously not all of the information is necessarily included; a low grade-point average, for example, is better omitted), making it complete but concise (*wrote press releases* instead of *my responsibilities included writing press releases*). Then the student should consider the arrangement of the sections on the page. Personal data and references are placed first and last respectively. Education is usually placed second, but those whose employment experience is stronger than their educational preparation may want to place the employment section second. In any event, the students should experiment with the use of spacing, capitalization, and underlining until they discover a format that adequately emphasizes their strengths.

Only after students have completed their resumés should they attempt a letter of application. Having analyzed their background and that of the company, they can better match their strengths with the requirements listed in the job description.

Like other business letters, the application letter follows a thesis-development-action structure, with the applicant's most persuasive qualifications offered on a single page. The first paragraph tells how the applicant learned of the job and why he or she is qualified for it by education and experience; the central strengths are identified at the outset. The second paragraph develops the education section of the thesis (including, perhaps, any research projects or seminars that are directly related to the position and that may or may not be included on the resumé). The third develops work experiences related to the position or to the qualities desired for the position. The concluding paragraph requests an interview. To discover more about the candidate than the one-page letter allows, the reader then refers to the resumé.

ACTIVITIES

1. Ask students to bring to class three business letters. Students may use ones they have received or, with permission, ones from their jobs. Have them work in small groups to analyze the format (the placement of the parts), the structure (thesis, development, action), spelling, and neatness of each. Ask students how their analyses affect their opinions of the company.

2. Suggest that students attend any resumé or interviewing workshop held by the Placement Office.

3. Ask someone from the Placement Office to talk to the class about the resumés students in the class have written. The instructor should submit copies well in advance so that the speaker can plan his or her comments and arrange for any necessary visual aids.

4. Ask students to write a letter requesting a letter of recommendation.

5. Invite the person in charge of hiring for a local business to share suggestions for an effective resumé.

6. Have students interview employers to discover the essentials of an effective letter and resumé as far as that company is concerned.

Criteria for Evaluating and Grading Themes

Knowing what letter grades symbolize helps both the instructor and the students. The instructor who adheres to clearly defined criteria (especially if the criteria are in use throughout the department) can concentrate on specific comments about the students' organization, development, and style rather than defend both the criteria and the comments every time a set of essays is returned. Students who understand that the criteria are a ready checklist as they revise also know that the degree to which the criteria are satisfied determines their grade; thus, they are confident of consistent standards from theme to theme. Finally, the use of such standards as those presented here makes clear the point that merely meeting the requirements of the assignment does not guarantee an A.

The following criteria deal with subject matter, style, use of rhetorical modes, organization, development, and mechanics. The final sentences of the A, B, and C paragraphs succinctly point out the differences in quality.*

A **paper:** Perhaps the principal characteristic of the A paper is its rich content. Some people describe the content as "meaty," others as "dense," still others as "packed." Whatever, the A paper demonstrates an excellent command of the subject matter. The information delivered is such that one feels significantly taught by the author, sentence after sentence, paragraph after paragraph. The A paper is also marked by stylistic finesse: the title and the opening paragraph are engaging; the transitions are artful; the phrasing is tight, fresh, and highly specific; the sentence structure is varied; the tone enhances the

---

*These grading criteria were written by John Trimble of the Department of English, The University of Texas, Austin, and are reprinted by permission.

purpose of the paper. The A paper shows an ability to explain, illustrate, compare, contrast, and synthesize ideas; it is consistently and adequately appropriate. Finally, the A paper, because of its careful organization and development, imparts a feeling of wholeness and unusual clarity. Not surprisingly, then, it leaves the reader feeling bright, thoroughly satisfied, and eager to reread the piece. In short, the A paper is organized, clear coherent, and effective throughout.

B **paper:** It is significantly more than competent. Besides being almost free of mechanical errors, the B paper delivers substantial information—that is, substantial in both quantity and interest. It demonstrates a good knowledge of the subject matter as well as a capacity for fluency of ideas and independent thinking, although not always realized in the paper. The specific points are logically ordered, well developed, and unified around a clear organizing principle that is apparent early in the paper. The ideas are usually adequately supported. The opening paragraph draws the reader in; the closing paragraph is both conclusive and thematically related to the opening. The transitions between paragraphs are for the most part smooth, the sentence structures pleasingly varied. The diction of the B paper is typically much more concise and precise than that found in the C paper. Occasionally, it even shows distinctiveness—i.e., finesse and memorability. On the whole, then, a B paper makes the reading experience a pleasurable one, for it offers substantial information with few distractions. In short, the writing in the B paper is organized, clear, coherent, and correct.

C **paper:** It is generally competent—it meets the assignment, has few mechanical errors, and is reasonably well organized and developed. The C paper demonstrates an average knowledge of the subject matter. The actual information it delivers, however, seems thin and commonplace. One reason for that impression is that the ideas are typically cast in the form of vague generalities—generalities that prompt the reader to ask marginally: "In every case?" "Exactly how large?" "Why?" "But how many?" The C paper reveals a weakness in effectively stating, explaining, and discussing ideas; the paper tends to be static—it does not "go anywhere." Stylistically, the C paper has other shortcomings as well: the opening paragraph does little to draw the reader in; the final paragraph offers only a perfunctory wrap-up; the transitions between paragraphs are often bumpy; the sentences, besides being choppy, tend to follow a predictable (hence monotonous) subject-verb-object order; the diction is occasionally marred by unconscious repetitions, redundancy, and imprecision. The C paper, then, while it accomplishes its purpose, lacks both imagination and intellectual rigor, and hence does not invite a rereading. The writing in the C paper is clear, controlled, and correct for the most part, but expression is occasionally faulty.

D paper: Its treatment and development of the subject are only rudimentary; the D paper demonstrates an inadequate grasp of the subject matter and fails to state, discuss, and develop ideas effectively. Ideas are inadequately supported. While organization is present, it is neither clear nor effective. Sentences are frequently awkward, ambiguous, and marred by serious mechanical errors. The writing is faulty: errors occur in mechanics (spelling, punctuation, run-on sentences, sentence fragments, subject-verb or pronoun-antecedent agreement); phrasing (awkward, unidiomatic, or ungrammatical sentences, inaccurate or inappropriate diction); organization (lack of paragraph logic, development, or unity). Evidence of careful proofreading is scanty, if it exists at all. In fact, the whole paper often gives the impression of having been conceived and written in haste.

F paper: Its treatment of the subject is superficial; its theme lacks discernible organization; its prose is garbled or stylistically primitive. The F paper manifests any or all of the qualities of the D theme. Errors in mechanics are frequent. The F paper fails to follow or to complete an assignment. In short, the ideas, organization, and style fall far below what is acceptable college writing.

Annotated Selective Bibliography

The results of research in the teaching of writing, both theory and application, are regularly found in the following journals. (An asterisk indicates a journal that publishes bibliographies of significant current articles.)

Basic Writing
College English Association Forum
Conference on Language Attitudes and Composition (CLAC)
* *College Composition and Communication*
College English
English Education
English Journal
Freshman English News
Language Arts
* *Research in the Teaching of English*
* *Rhetoric Society Quarterly*
Style
Teaching English in the Two-Year College
Writing as a Liberating Activity Newsletter

Throughout this bibliography the bracketed numbers refer to related sections in the *Harbrace College Handbook*. A bullet (•) precedes titles that are considered required reading for all teachers of composition.

BIBLIOGRAPHIES AND BIBLIOGRAPHICAL ESSAYS

Bennett, James R. et al. "The Paragraph: An Annotated Bibliography," *Style*, 11 (Spring 1977), 107–18. ◊ Includes references on structure, the process of paragraphing, and the relation of the paragraph to the entire work. [**31**]

Cooper, Charles R. and Lee Odell, eds. *Research on Composing: Points of Departure.* Urbana, Ill.: National Council of Teachers of English, 1978. ◊ An anthology that includes selections by such researchers as Janet Emig, James Britton, and Donald Murray.

Dieterich, Daniel J. and Richard H. Behm. "Annotated Bibliography of Research in the Teaching of English," *Research in the Teaching of English.* ◊ Appearing twice yearly in the May and December issues, the bibliography annotates research in bilingual/bidialectal studies; language and verbal learning; literature, humanities, and media; teacher education; testing and evaluation; written and oral communication. Bibliographies prior to 1979 are by Dieterich.

Larson, Richard L. "Selected Bibliography of Research and Writing About the Teaching of Composition," *College Composition and Communication.* ◊ Annual annotated bibliography first published in May 1975.

————. "Selected Bibliography of Writings on the Evaluation of Students' Achievements in Composition." *Journal of Basic Writing,* 1 (Spring–Summer 1978), 91–100. ◊ Annotations of articles focused on evaluating or responding to students' writing.

Tate, Gary, ed. *Teaching Composition: Ten Bibliographical Essays.* Fort Worth: Texas Christian University Press, 1976. ◊ A collection of essays on topics central to the teaching of writing. Includes essays on invention, structure and form, style, modes of discourse, basic writing, uses of media, linguistics, rhetorical analysis, dialects, and fields related to composition.

THEORY

Britton, James et al. *The Development of Writing Abilities (11–18).* London: Collier Macmillan, 1975. ◊ Reports on research project; bases a classification system of writing on both function and audience.

D'Angelo, Frank. *A Conceptual Theory of Rhetoric.* Cambridge, Mass.: Winthrop, 1975. ◊ Proposes a theory of linguistic and rhetorical principles that "determine the intrinsic nature of discourse." Context and essential characteristics of rhetoric examined in an effort to "explore the relationships that exist between thinking and writing, within the framework of a coherent theoretical system of rhetoric."

Emig, Janet. "Writing as a Mode of Learning." *College Composition and Communication,* 28 (May 1977), 122–28. ◊ Contends writing is a "unique mode of learning" and contrasts writing with talking. Outlines parallels between writing and successful learning strategies. [**32**]

- Hirsch, E. D., Jr. *The Philosophy of Composition.* Chicago: University of Chicago Press, 1977. ◇ Believes readability should be the major stylistic concern in both teaching and evaluation. Chapter 6 (''Some Practical Implications'') offers suggestions to improve teaching methods.
- Kinneavy, James L. *A Theory of Discourse.* Englewood Cliffs, N. J.: Prentice-Hall, 1971. ◇ Detailed, systematic study of reference, persuasive, literary, and expressive discourse. [**32**]
- Moffett, James. *Teaching the Universe of Discourse.* Boston: Houghton Mifflin, 1968. ◇ Discussion of the author's discourse theory based on speaker, audience, and subject. Shows parallels between discourse and levels of abstraction. Drama and narrative discourse examined in particular detail. Points out the strengths and weaknesses of transformational grammar, sentence combining, and textbooks. [**31, 32**]
- Winterowd, W. Ross, ed. *Contemporary Rhetoric: A Conceptual Background with Readings.* New York: Harcourt, 1975. ◇ A collection of twenty-four essays on invention, form, and style. Interprets recent work on rhetoric and establishes the direction of future work. Introductory essay by the editor.

APPROACHES AND STRATEGIES

Coles, William. *Composing: Writing as a Self-Creating Process.* Rochelle Park, N. J.: Hayden, 1974. ◇ Presents thirty cases or problems.

———. *The Plural I: The Teaching of Writing.* New York: Holt, 1978. ◇ An account of how students in a composition class move from being students who write themes to writers who recognize the power of their voices.

- Corbett, Edward P. J. *Classical Rhetoric for the Modern Student.* 2nd ed. New York: Oxford University Press, 1971. ◇ Presents the three essential units of classical rhetoric: invention, arrangement, and style. Emphasizes argument. [**23**]

D'Angelo, Frank. ''Advertising and the Modes of Discourse.'' *College Composition and Communication,* 29 (December 1978), 356–61. ◇ Examines ads as examples of descriptive, narrative, and expository-argumentative modes. Includes a checklist of six suggestions for using advertising to teach forms of discourse. [**32**]

Donovan, Timothy and Ben W. McClelland, eds. *Eight Approaches to*

Teaching Composition. Urbana, Ill.: National Council of Teachers of English, 1980. ◊ Collection that includes essays on rhetorical, epistemic, and revised-models approaches as well as essays on basic writing, conference, and across-the-curriculum approaches.

Elbow, Peter. *Writing Without Teachers.* New York: Oxford University Press, 1975. ◊ Focuses on invention in free writing; advises reader-writer how to benefit from the process of reacting to writing. Explains how to set up a "teacherless" course.

Flower, Linda. *Problem-Solving Strategies for Writing.* New York: Harcourt, 1981. ◊ Brings together the rhetorical topics (invention, arrangement, and style) and a process approach to writing in order to show how an awareness of intellectual processes affects a writer's strategies.

Graves, Richard L., ed. *Rhetoric and Composition: A Sourcebook for Teachers.* Rochelle Park, N. J.: Hayden, 1976. ◊ Anthology of articles from professional journals. Emphasis on motivating writers, teaching the sentence and the paragraph, using classical rhetoric. One section is devoted to techniques of teaching. Authors include Cooper, Christensen, Becker, Larson, Berthoff, Corbett, and Winterowd.

Hoffman, Eleanor M. and John P. Schifsky. "Designing Writing Assignments." *English Journal,* 66 (December 1977), 41–45. ◊ Suggests that writing assignments should specify the aim, mode, audience, and purpose of the discourse. Three sets of satisfactory and unsatisfactory assignments are included. [**31, 32, 34**]

Irmscher, William F. *Teaching Expository Writing.* New York: Holt, 1979. ◊ Practical guidance on organizing a course along with instruction on teaching mechanics, style, structure. Includes assignments and activities. Analyzes the qualities (content, form, diction, mechanics, and style) of A, B, and C essays with less attention to D and E essays.

Koch, Carl and James M. Brazil. *Strategies for Teaching the Composition Process.* Urbana, Ill.: National Council of Teachers of English, 1978. ◊ Presents resources and strategies for a student-centered, process-oriented writing class. In addition to instructions for pre-writing, writing, and post-writing stages, the authors include a section on helping students overcome writing anxieties.

Macrorie, Ken. *Telling Writing.* Rochelle Park, N. J.: Hayden, 1970. ◊ A free-writing program in which students gain a knowledge of their own writing voices as well as the enthusiasm and ways of professional writers.

McKeachie, Wilbert J. *Teaching Tip·: A Guide-Book for the Beginning College Teacher.* 7th ed. Lexington, Mass.: D. C. Heath, 1978. ◊ Discusses the how to's of preparing to teach a course, meeting a class for the first time, leading discussion, and evaluating students' progress. Appendices include an evaluation form for teachers and a checklist of teaching techniques.

Murray, Donald M. *A Writer Teaches Writing: A Practical Method of Teaching Composition.* Boston: Houghton Mifflin, 1968. ◊ In addition to presenting a method of teaching composition, offers sample lesson plans and advice on designing and evaluating assignments. Myths of teaching composition, a collection of quotations from writers on writing, and an extensive bibliography of works for the teacher's library are also included.

Ohmann, Richard M. and W. B. Coley, eds. *Ideas for Teaching English 101: Teaching Writing in College.* Urbana, Ill.: National Council of Teachers of English, 1975. ◊ Reprints twenty-three articles from *College English,* March 1967–January 1975. Essays covering methods, theories, models, and suggestions are written by such authors as Bruffee, Winterowd, Wiener, Macrorie, Mandel, and Comprone.

Winterowd, W. Ross. *The Contemporary Writer.* 2nd ed. New York: Harcourt, 1981. ◊ Shows how much of the theory works out in classroom practice.

Young, Richard E., Alton L. Becker, and Kenneth L. Pike. *Rhetoric: Discovery and Change.* New York: Harcourt, 1970. ◊ Discusses the making of choices in writing by applying six maxims derived from tagmemics. See Chapter 14 for a discussion of revision.

WRITING ABOUT LITERATURE   [32, 33]

Roberts, Edgar V. *Writing Themes About Literature.* 4th ed. Englewood Cliffs, N. J.: Prentice-Hall, 1977. ◊ Specific guidelines for writing and organizing papers of summary, analysis (for example, character, point of view, structure, imagery, tone), evaluation, and review. Includes sample themes for each type of assignment.

Rohrberger, Mary and Samuel H. Woods, Jr. *Reading and Writing About Literature.* New York: Random House, 1971. ◊ Provides context by introducing genre, critical approaches, and critical vocabulary. Discusses thesis, introductions, primary and secondary sources.

THE RESEARCH PAPER [33]

Katz, William. *Your Library: A Reference Guide.* New York: Holt, 1979. ◊ Explains to the beginning researcher how to use the library's resources and then how to locate sources in the humanities, science, social sciences. Useful charts key research questions to appropriate resources. Title index includes Library of Congress and Dewey Decimal numbers for every resource mentioned in the book.

Turabian, Kate L. *A Manual for Writers of Term Papers, Theses, and Dissertations.* 4th ed. Chicago: University of Chicago Press, Phoenix Books, 1973. ◊ Manual of style for both scientific and non-scientific formal papers. Directions on format, organization, and mechanics of typing.

Winkler, Anthony C. and Jo Ray McCuen. *Writing the Research Paper: A Handbook.* New York: Harcourt, 1979. ◊ Based on the 1977 *MLA Handbook*, it includes annotated lists of general and specialized references as well as a guide to writing about literature.

ARGUMENTATION

Kneupper, Charles W. "Teaching Argument: An Introduction to the Toulmin Model." *College Composition and Communication,* 29 (October 1978), 237–41. ◊ Explains the model of argument now used in speech instruction and applies it to paragraph one of Thoreau's "Civil Disobedience" to illustrate its usefulness in discourse analysis. The model consists of six elements: data, warrant, claim, qualifier, reservation, backing. [**23, 32**]

Weddle, Perry. *Argument: A Guide to Critical Thinking.* New York: McGraw-Hill, 1977. ◊ Seven chapters explaining and illustrating such subjects as fallacy, authority, cause, connotation, and definition. [**19, 23, 31**]

EVALUATION

Cooper, Charles R. and Lee Odell, eds. *Evaluating Writing: Describing, Measuring, Judging.* Urbana, Ill.: National Council of Teachers of English, 1977. ◊ Six essays on measuring and evaluating growth in writing plus an introduction by the editors. Topics include holistic scoring, syntactic maturity, and approaches to evaluation.

- Diederich, Paul B. *Measuring Growth in English.* Urbana, Ill.: National Council of Teachers of English, 1974. ◊ Outlines a system of staff grading; also includes topics for essay tests, a thirty-four-item test on knowledge of grammar, and a discussion on the harm of excessive correction.

  Krishna, Valerie. "The Syntax of Error." *Journal of Basic Writing,* 1 (Spring 1975), 43–49. ◊ To help students overcome problems of illogical syntax, recommends having them locate main ideas in subjects and verbs. [**1, 24, 29**]

  Lloyd-Jones, Richard. "Primary Trait Scoring." In *Evaluating Writing: Describing, Measuring, Judging.* Eds. Charles R. Cooper and Lee Odell. Urbana, Ill.: National Council of Teachers of English, 1977, 33–66. ◊ Explains steps in primary trait scoring: defining the "universe of discourse" and developing exercises for it, securing the writers' cooperation, developing and using workable scoring guides. Two writing tasks along with their scoring guides illustrate the evaluation of students' discourse.

- Shaughnessy, Mina P. *Errors and Expectations: A Guide for the Teacher of Basic Writing.* New York: Oxford University Press, 1977. ◊ Analyzes range of writing problems, offers explanations for the occurrence of the problems, and suggests ways to handle the problems. Includes outlines of sample lessons, a sequence of lessons on verbs, and teaching activities. Discusses handwriting and punctuation, syntax, common errors, spelling, vocabulary, and elements beyond the sentence. Also provides a chart of writing skills to help in the planning of a composition sequence, an appendix of topics for placement essays, and an annotated bibliography.

THE PROCESS:
PREWRITING AND INVENTION

  Adams, James L. *Conceptual Blockbusting: A Guide to Better Ideas.* San Francisco: W. H. Freeman, 1974. ◊ The director of the Design Laboratory at Stanford University discusses problem-solving and heuristics in an accessible and interesting way.

- Emig, Janet. *The Composing Processes of Twelfth Graders.* NCTE Research Report No. 13. Urbana, Ill.: National Council of Teachers of English, 1971. ◊ Reports on the case study of the composing processes used by eight twelfth-grade students. Finds that the characteristics of "self-sponsored" writing include peers as the selected audience, subjects from all fields, no "written prefiguring," stopping during the process, occasional contemplative pauses, and fairly ready revision. Behavior for "school-sponsored" writing, on the other hand, differs in the categories of context, stimuli, pre-writing, stopping, contemplation, and voluntary revision. [**31, 32**]

Flower, Linda and John R. Hayes. "The Cognition of Discovery: Defining a Rhetorical Problem." *College Composition and Communication,* 31 (February 1980), 21–32. ◊ Defines discovery as "an act of making meaning . . . in response to a *self-defined problem* or goal" and charts the elements of a rhetorical problem (rhetorical situation and writer's personal goals). Observes that good writers "respond to *all* aspects of the rhetorical problem," "create a particularly rich network of goals for affecting their reader," and "represent the problem not only in more breadth, but in depth." [**31, 32**]

————. "Problem-Solving Strategies and the Writing Process." *College English,* 39 (December 1977), 449–61. ◊ Recommends problem-solving approach and outlines in detail a heuristic strategy for analytical writing. Notes that while problem-solving approach does not yield ready-made steps to producing discourse, it does acknowledge the workings of the thought process. [**31, 32**]

Larson, Richard L. "Problem-Solving, Composing and Liberal Education." *College English,* 33 (March 1972), 628–35. ◊ Applies eight steps of problem-solving to Swift's "A Modest Proposal" as part of his demonstration that problem-solving is a strategy for defining, organizing, and evaluating complex arguments. [**23, 31, 32**]

Rohman, D. Gordon. "Pre-Writing: The Stage of Discovery in the Writing Process." *College Composition and Communication,* 16 (May 1965), 106–12. ◊ Suggests journals, principles of religious meditation, and analogy as ways to help students define a subject and a context for their writing. [**32**]

THE PROCESS:
WRITING AND ARRANGEMENT [**31, 32**]

Baker, Sheridan. *The Practical Stylist.* 5th ed. New York: Crowell, 1980. ◊ Begins with the thesis statement, moving then to paragraph structure and the sentence. Home of the "argumentative edge" and "funnel paragraph." With exercises.

Larson, Richard L. "Toward a Linear Rhetoric of the Essay." *College Composition and Communication,* 22 (May 1971), 140–46. ◊ Argues for a linear plan to complement hierarchical models of discourse. The plan is based on five propositions: that the essay is made up of a series of steps, that "similar overall plans . . . organize many different essays," that an essay may include more than one plan, that the selection of a plan or plans influences the reader's reaction to the discussion, and that the selection of a plan or plans "probably determines in large part the data and materials."

Winterowd, W. Ross. "The Grammar of Coherence." *College English,* 31 (May 1970), 828–35. ◊ Argues that there is a grammar of coherent discourse and that the grammar is composed of seven relationships: coordination, obversativity, causativity, conclusivity, alternativity, inclusivity, and sequence.

THE PROCESS: STYLE

Joos, Martin. *The Five Clocks.* New York: Harcourt, Harbinger Books, 1967. ◊ Introduction to the five styles of English: frozen, formal, consultative, casual, and intimate. [**19, 27, 32**]

Strunk, William, Jr. and E. B. White. *The Elements of Style.* 3rd ed. New York: Macmillan, 1978. ◊ Four chapters concentrate on the most frequent errors of usage; in the fifth White adds his views on style.

Williams, Joseph. *Style: Ten Lessons in Clarity and Grace.* Glenview, Ill.: Scott, Foresman, 1981. ◊ The single best work on accessibility (the relative readability of prose).

THE PROCESS: REVISION

Sommers, Nancy. "Revision Strategies of Student Writers and Experienced Adult Writers." *College Composition and Communication,* 31 (December 1980), 378–88. ◊ A case study using twenty student writers and twenty experienced writers shows that student writers view revising as a matter of rewording. Students have strategies for the word and sentence levels but not for the essay as a whole. Experienced writers revise to define meaning and to meet the anticipated judgment of an audience; they have strategies for all levels and see revision as a recursive, holistic process. While students force their essays to meet narrowly defined rules given them by instructors, experienced writers create meaning as they write. [**20, 23, 25, 29, 31, 32**]

Lanham, Richard A. *Revising Business Prose.* New York: Scribner's, 1981. ◊ Lanham's eight-step Paramedic Method from *Revis-*

ing Prose (1978) applied to the prose of business and government. Section on Official Style includes Philip Broughton's "Systematic Buzz Phrase Projector." **[19, 21]**

DICTION AND USAGE

Algeo, John. *Problems in the Origins and Development of the English Language.* 2nd ed. New York: Harcourt, 1972 (3rd ed., 1983). ◊ Contains information on OED and early dictionaries in Chapters 1 and 8. Examples of lexical and semantic change in Chapters 10 and 12. **[5, 7, 15, 19]**

Newman, Edwin. *Strictly Speaking: Will America Be the Death of English?* Indianapolis: Bobbs-Merrill, 1974. ◊ Uses many illustrations from politics, education, journalism, advertising, sports, and gastronomy to support the thesis that language mirrors society and to argue for lucid English. **[19–21]**

Pyles, Thomas. *The Origins and Development of the English Language.* 2nd ed. New York: Harcourt, 1971 (3rd ed., with John Algeo, 1983). ◊ Systematically traces the phonological, grammatical, and syntactic changes in English. Chapters 10 ("New Words from Old: Coinages and Adaptations") and 12 ("Words and Meanings") catalog methods of lexical and semantic change. **[19]**

Shuy, Roger W. *Discovering American Dialects.* Urbana, Ill.: National Council of Teachers of English, 1967. ◊ Brief general guide to the field of dialectology. Items and checklist of the phonology, grammar, and lexicon of regional dialects. **[19]**

THE SENTENCE

Christensen, Francis. "A Generative Rhetoric of the Sentence." *College Composition and Communication,* 14 (October 1963), 155–61. ◊ Defines the four principles of a generative rhetoric of the sentence as addition, direction of movement, levels of generality or abstraction, and texture. Recommends Paul Roberts' *English Sentences* (Harcourt, 1962) as the grammar to clarify levels of syntax. Sees a shift in prose away from the complex sentence to the cumulative sentence. Examples included. **[1, 24, 25, 29, 30]**

Daiker, Donald, Andrew Kerek, and Max Morenberg. *The Writer's Options: College Sentence Combining.* New York: Harper & Row, 1979. ◊ Eighteen units of exercises designed to show students the varieties of structures (such as participles, absolutes, relative clauses) and strategies (such as emphasis, coherence, tone) available to writers. Also a chapter showing how a controlling idea (topic sentence) determines the content and organization of a paragraph. [**1, 25, 27, 29, 31**]

Graves, Richard L. "Levels of Skill in the Composing Process." *College Composition and Communication,* 29 (October 1978), 227–32. ◊ Explains the mental processes involved in three progressively more complex activities: combining kernel sentences, revising flawed sentences, and composing sentences based on rhetorical models. [**24–26, 29, 30**]

Hunt, Kellogg W. *Grammatical Structures Written at Three Grade Levels.* NCTE Research Report No. 3. Champaign, Ill.: National Council of Teachers of English, 1965. ◊ Reports findings of a study on the writing of fifty-four students, each writing approximately one thousand words. Concludes that length of independent clauses (T-units) is related to maturity: the writing of adults contains longer T-units than those in twelfth graders' writing. [**24–26, 29, 30**]

———. *Syntactic Maturity in Schoolchildren and Adults.* Monographs of the Society for Research in Child Development, No. 134. Chicago: University of Chicago Press, 1970. ◊ Reports findings of a study of writing done by more than one thousand students (grades 4, 6, 8, and 10) asked to rewrite the "aluminum passage," thirty-two short sentences. Finds that older students write longer T-units, use more strategies for revision, and add meanings as they revise. [**24–26, 29, 30**]

Mellon, John C. *Transformational Sentence-Combining: A Method for Enhancing the Development of Syntactic Fluency in English Composition.* NCTE Research Report No. 10. Champaign, Ill.: National Council of Teachers of English, 1969. ◊ Reports on a one-year experiment in which sentence-combining (without instruction in transformational rules) was taught as part of seventh graders' unit in linguistics; finds a significant increase in syntactic fluency. [**24–26, 29, 30**]

O'Hare, Frank. *Sentence Combining: Improving Student Writing Without Formal Grammar Instruction.* NCTE Research Report No. 15. Urbana, Ill.: National Council of Teachers of English, 1973. ◊ Reports growth in syntactic maturity of seventh graders when sentence-combining is taught without introducing the terminology of transformational grammar. [**24–26, 29, 30**]

Pence, R. W. and D. W. Emery. *A Grammar of Present-Day English.* 2nd ed. New York: Macmillan, 1963. ◊ A detailed grammar of English using the traditional approach. [**1, 6, 7**]

Rippon, Michelle and Walter E. Meyers. *Combining Sentences.* New York: Harcourt, 1979. ◊ After a quick review of sentence types and parts of speech, thirty-four lessons give students abundant practice in combining with the use of simple signals and instructions. A final section is devoted to planning and writing a paragraph.

Roberts, Paul. *English Sentences.* New York: Harcourt, 1962. ◊ Early transformational-generative grammar still useful for its classification of sentence patterns. [**1**]

Strong, William. "Sentence Combining: Back to the Basics and Beyond." *English Journal,* 65 (February 1976), 56, 60–64. ◊ Stresses sentence-combining as a means to develop linguistic options. Outlines advantages of sentence-combining, presents examples of signaled and open exercises, recommends procedures for using them in the classroom.

THE PARAGRAPH

Christensen, Francis. *Notes Toward a New Rhetoric: Nine Essays for Teachers.* 2nd ed. New York: Harper & Row, 1978. ◊ A collection of essays on the structure of the sentence and the paragraph. [**21, 23–26, 29, 30, 31**]

————. "A Generative Rhetoric of the Paragraph." *College Composition and Communication,* 16 (October 1965), 144–56. ◊ Four principles that guide the rhetoric of the sentence are here applied to the paragraph. Each of nine characteristics of the paragraph is discussed. [**31**]

———— and Bonniejean Christensen. *A New Rhetoric.* New York: Harper & Row, 1976. ◊ Proceeds from a generative rhetoric of the sentence, emphasizing the cumulative sentence and beginning with description-narration, then moves to the paragraph and expository essays. [**21, 23–26, 29–31**]

SEMANTICS

Chase, Stuart. *The Tyranny of Words.* New York: Harcourt, Harvest Books, 1966. ◊ Introduction to semantics. Includes examples of language abuse by economists and politicians. [**19–21**]

Hayakawa, S. I. *Language in Thought and Action.* 4th ed. New York: Harcourt, 1978. ◊ Introduction to semantics. Includes chapters on report, inference, and judgment; context; connotation; metaphor and simile; definition; classification. [**19, 23, 31**]

Annotated
Sample Pages

The following sample pages from the *Harbrace College Workbook,*
Forms 9A and 9C, are provided here to help instructors decide whether
to order examination copies of these workbooks from the publisher.
(These pages are reduced from their actual size—7" by 9".)

1 Correction symbols and section numbers correspond to those in the Handbook.

2 Directives are simply expressed.

3 As in the Handbook, cross-references are generously supplied.

4 Each Workbook has its own theme, used throughout—in this case, sports.

5 The explanatory material addresses real problems while avoiding condescension.

Comma Splice and Fused Sentence   cs/fs 3   1

3

Learn the standard ways to link two closely related main clauses.   2

In Section **1** you studied the two main ways to expand a sentence—subordination and coordination. Subordination often requires the use of a comma or commas for the subordinated addition to the main clause. (See also **12b** and **12d**.)   3

Coordination, too, requires a comma when two main clauses are connected by a coordinating conjunction—*and*, *but*, *or*, *nor*, and *for*.

> Most people think that hang gliding is a new sport, *but* it actually dates back to the eleventh century.

If the coordinating conjunction is removed, the two main clauses may still be connected; however, the standard mark of punctuation between the two clauses then becomes the semicolon.

> Most people think that hang gliding is a new sport; it actually dates back to the eleventh century.

Even if another type of connective—a conjunctive adverb like *then*, *therefore*, or *however*—is inserted between the main clauses, a semicolon is still the standard mark of punctuation to be used after the first main clause.   4

> Most people think that hang gliding is a new sport; *however*, it actually dates back to the eleventh century.

If a comma is used between two main clauses not connected by a coordinating conjunction, the sentence contains a *comma splice*. In other words, the comma has been made to perform a function that standard usage has not given it.

> COMMA SPLICE   Most people think that hang gliding is a new sport, it actually dates back to the eleventh century.
> COMMA SPLICE   Most people think that hang gliding is a new sport, however, it actually dates back to the eleventh century.

Some students feel they can avoid comma splices by omitting all commas from their writing. And they are right. But in so doing they violate standard practices of punctuation even further. Instead of writing comma-splice sentences, they write *fused* (or run-together) sentences. And fused sentences are even more ineffective than comma-splice sentences because they are difficult to understand at first reading.   5

> FUSED SENTENCE   The first known person to hang glide was an English monk using a crude form of a hang glider he took off from a sixty-foot tower.

1 A sample exercise and sample written answer are included at the beginning of each exercise set.

2 The sports theme continues—informative as well as engaging.

3 All pages are perforated. When the exercise pages are detached, the explanatory material remains, serving as a sort of mini-handbook.

FORM 9A

COMMA SPLICE AND FUSED SENTENCE

Comma splices and fused sentences   Exercise 3–1

NAME _____ SCORE_____

DIRECTIONS In each of the following sentences insert an inverted caret ($\vee$) between main clauses. Then indicate in the first blank at the right whether the sentence is correctly punctuated according to standard practice (*C*), contains a comma splice (*CS*), or is fused (*F*). Correct each error by the method you consider best, showing in the second blank whether you have used subordination (*sub*), a period (*.*), a semicolon (*;*), or a comma plus a coordinating conjunction (*conj*).

EXAMPLE

Socrates argued that sports were necessary for the full de-

velopment of the human being $\vee$ he felt, however, that an

overemphasis on sports would produce an insensitive

human being.   F   ;

1. One of the dialogues in Plato's *Republic* takes place between Socrates and Glaucon the two discuss the effects of gymnastics and music on the development of a human being. _____ _____

2. Gymnastics (in modern terms, sports) makes a person strong and brave, on the other hand, music (in modern terms, the arts) makes a person sensitive and gentle, Socrates argued. _____ _____

3. Training in both gymnastics and music is required to produce the ideal human being, the two areas work together to make a person both strong and sensitive. _____ _____

4. Without training in gymnastics a person would be too soft, without training in music a person would be too fierce. _____ _____

5. "I am quite aware that the mere athlete becomes too much of a savage," said Socrates, "the mere musician is melted and softened beyond what is good for him." _____ _____

6. In the *Republic* Plato described an ideal state, such a state would be made up of well-rounded human beings. _____ _____

1 The theme of Form 9C is the world of work.

2 New to Form 9C is the inclusion of a documented report.

BUSINESS WRITING

33c Learn to write a report.

Businesses require reports for a variety of purposes: to describe mechanisms and processes; to provide instructions; to relate progress on the development of products or procedures; to analyze systems and procedures; to present proposals; and to record trips, minutes of meetings, and accidents. Most of these types of reports have been discussed in the exercise material of this workbook.

1

(1) Learn to write a process analysis.

Most reports that you are likely to write will be developed by process analysis, a step-by-step explanation of how something is made, how it works, or how it is done. You may practice this kind of report by writing a process analysis of something you are familiar with. What follows is a process analysis of how a thermometer works.

How a Thermometer Works

There is no instrument the American home depends
on more than the thermometer. On a winter day, for
example, the thermometer tells us how cold it is out-
side or how warm inside, whether or not we have a fever from
our winter cold, when the roast in our oven is done, and
if the chocolate mixture on the stove has reached the
soft-ball stage. Whether it is a thermometer out-
side our door, a thermostat on our furnace, or a
thermometer in our mouth, our meat, or our candy, the
same process is at work to show us how hot or cold
something is.

2

A thermometer is usually a glass tube with a small
bulb at the end. The bulb contains a liquid, either
mercury or alcohol, that rises or falls inside the glass
tube. The tube has degree markings that show how much
the liquid has risen or fallen: the higher the liquid

NOTES